THE BOTTOM OF THE FOX

A True Story of Love, Devotion
& Cold-Blooded Murder

By SHAUN D. MULLEN

ISBN 1-4537-7404-1

HV6534 .D44 M8x 2010
Murder - Pennsylvania - Delaware Water Gap

© 2002-2010 by Shaun D. Mullen
and Fishy Business Press

All rights are reserved. Except for brief quotations
in a review, this book may not be produced in any form
without the written permission of the author.

First edition published in April 2010
Second edition published in September 2010

Printed in the United States of America

Cover photograph of Phil Woods and Eddie Joubert
at the 1981 Delaware Water Gap Celebration of the Arts
© 1981 Walter Bredel

"The Thrill Is Gone" lyrics © 1951 Rick Darnell and Roy Hawkin

… The Bottom of the Fox

CONTENTS

Foreward & Acknowledgements

Notes on the Second Edition

Chapter One: What the Barred Owl Saw 1

Chapter Two: Of Lenapes & Land Grabs 15

Chapter Three: The Hiker 29

Chapter Four: Down By the River 36

Chapter Five: America Starts Here 50

Chapter Six: Those Baleful Brown Eyes 63

Chapter Seven: He's Dead, We Checked 71

Chapter Eight: The Getaway 78

Chapter Nine: Darkness, Darkness 85

Chapter Ten: The Ax Fell Off the Roof 97

Chapter Eleven: The Awful Something 107

Chapter Twelve: He Found Himself Adrift 116

Chapter Thirteen: All Hail Caesar! 125

Chapter Fourteen: The Hiker Returns 131

Afterword 139

Appendices 149

About the Author

FOREWARD
and ACKNOWLEDGEMENTS

A few months after Eddie Joubert was murdered at the Bottom of the Fox, his bar in the village of Delaware Water Gap in the Pocono Mountains of Northeastern Pennsylvania, a friend went to work for the organizers of a jazz festival that he had helped start. Although Eddie was an integral part of the festival and the Gap community, my friend said that he never once heard anyone mention him while he was associated with the event.

Eddie had been dead for 21 years when I began research for *The Bottom of the Fox: A True Story of Love, Devotion and Cold-Blooded Murder*. That's a long time, but I too soon learned that people had quickly put aside the horrifying events of November 28, 1981.

While festival veterans dispute my friend's claim, I also concluded that people had boxed up and put away their memories of Eddie. After all, that is only human. Yet as Jodie Hutton, chief deputy coroner of Monroe County, Pennsylvania puts it, "Guilt is a debt that you never pay off," and two decades did not diminish the guilt some people expressed when I told them I was writing a book about Eddie.

They hadn't opened their Eddie boxes in years and felt guilty about that. They felt guilty because they wondered if there was anything they could have done to prevent his death. They felt guilty because they knew that Cheryl Joubert, his oldest child and torch bearer, might have gotten more support from the friends her father so valued as she struggled with the awfulness of his death while trying to keep the Fox open. They felt guilty because they hadn't pressed the Pennsylvania State Police harder to try to find the killer.

Underlying their guilt is the fact that Eddie had touched their lives in ways few others had. He judged people not by who they were -- indeed, his friends ranged from world famous jazz and folk musicians to troubled and sometimes homeless Vietnam War veterans who lived hand-to-mouth existences -- but by their goodness. He was easygoing, but had a shooting-out-sparks incandescence. He was apolitical, but had a passion for important and sometimes unpopular causes. He was not book smart, but inhaled and analyzed information like a sage elder. He was irreligious, but deeply spiritual.

Back in the day, Eddie and two of those musicians -- trombonist Rick Chamberlain and alto saxophonist Phil Woods -- were known as the "Unholy Three." They came up with the idea of the jazz festival as a way to raise money to fix the Gap's decrepit sewer system on a boozy night on the front porch of the Deer Head Inn jazz club in 1978. Chamberlain, who Eddie later talked into successfully running for Gap village council, which in turn jumpstarted a lifelong dedication to community service, was eager to talk to me.

"That was such a formative part of our lives," said Chamberlain. "The spirit of Eddie's life needs to be rekindled."

Folk singer Rosalie Sorrels recalled the first time she met Eddie:

"It was like I already knew him just from his smile and the eye contact, which is what makes music and human love work.

"Good of you to bring him back," she told me. "We need him now more than ever."

Serendipitously, my introduction to Eddie came on the opening day of the 2002 jazz festival, which is formally known as the Delaware Water Gap Celebration of the Arts (COTA).

I picked up an old festival program from a freebie bin and

was thumbing through it between acts. On a back page was the marvelous Walter Bredel photograph gracing the cover of this book. Eddie and Woods are looking out from the festival stage at a standing room-only crowd. Both are wearing festival t-shirts and copies of Woods' trademark Sundance Leather driving cap. A pack of Camels peeks out of a pocket of Eddie's vest. He has a plastic drink cup in his right hand, probably filled with beer, and a big grin on his face.

"I had just told Eddie that he was to blame for all of this," Woods told me with a chuckle as we looked at the photograph many years later.

I knew of Woods before I interviewed him for *The Bottom of the Fox*. He is near or at the top of every list of great alto sax players and his "Song for Sisyphus" is a longtime personal favorite. I didn't recognize the guy standing next to him, however, although that incandescence leaped off the page.

I asked my friend who the other man was.

"Oh, that's Eddie Joubert," she replied.

I asked what instrument he played.

"He wasn't a musician."

"Who is he?"

"He owned a bar down the hill, the Bottom of the Fox. He helped start the festival."

"I'd like to meet him. Can you introduce me?"

My friend paused. "Um, that's not possible."

It also is only human to treat what happened to Eddie as an isolated act of depravity that had no connection to other crimes. Although this book will show otherwise, people took comfort in that fiction.

Robbie Rosenblum, a criminal attorney who knew "Edward," as he called Eddie, about as well as anyone outside of his immediate family, made that point at our first meeting. "People want to put the murder behind them," Rosenblum explained. "They don't want to reopen old wounds. They don't want to wonder whether there's still an ax murderer out there. I sometimes feel that way myself."

As we got up from lunch at one of Rosenblum's watering holes, I told him that I hoped we could talk some more.

"I seriously doubt that's going to happen," he said. Talking about Eddie had depressed him.

As it turned out, we got together a dozen more times before Rosenblum's death on the eve of the 2003 jazz festival. Rosenblum opened his Eddie box big time, perhaps because he knew that his run of martini lunches was nearing an end. But I believe it was more than that. Like Eddie, Rosenblum was a fierce defender of the underdog.

I became determined to get to know the man whom I had seen in only a single photograph, and the result is *The Bottom of the Fox*.

The world needs another book about an unsolved murder like Barack Obama needs another war. *The Bottom of the Fox* is indeed the story of Eddie's death, but it is much more: It is the story of his life, the extended family he so cherished, and the turbulent times in which he lived. It also is the first book that provides an unvarnished look at the Poconos, a unique but troubled area that Eddie had fallen deeply in love with that is typically portrayed as a four-season Eden as does Lawrence Squeri in his *Better in the Poconos*.

With nary a discouraging word, Squeri's book is a tourist bureau's wet dream; *The Bottom of the Fox* is most definitely not and explores in detail why things have gotten so seriously off message in a once special place.

My journalistic cherry was broken in the late 1960s, a time when newspaper editors and reporters were, with few exceptions, scrupulously honest and tried hard to be objective, as well as chain smokers who kept a pint of rye or gin in a desk drawer to lubricate their prose before the next deadline. *The Bottom of the Fox* hopefully reflects those values, but it is lumbering onto the stage at a time when deadlines have been atomized by the Internet and the 24/7 world in which we live. One consequence is that the "truth" has become a malleable good.

Although this book is an accurate recounting of events based on hundreds of hours of interviews and hundreds more of research, minor elements of the story have been altered. By necessity, a very few names have been left out or changed to protect certain individuals' privacy, while the thoughts and words of some people have been reconstructed since Eddie and other key players are long dead.

Considerable effort went into rendering those reconstructions as accurately as possible based on the recollections of Eddie's friends, official records such as they are, and other contemporary accounts.

Sincere thanks are due the many people who opened their Eddie boxes for me. Only a very small number of people refused to talk once word got around about my endeavor.

I also am indebted to Zachary Stalberg, the legendary former editor of the Philadelphia *Daily News*, who recognized that I had a book in me, as well as Ellen Foley, his managing editor at the time of my retirement, without whose encouragement I might not have left the newspaper business, and to Dave Brown of Horse Cow Designs, who helped design the print and Web versions of this book. But thanks most especially are due a dear friend of many years whose commitment to me and to Eddie's legacy made this a much better book. She got me through to the finish line.

SHAUN D. MULLEN
April 2010

NOTES ON THE SECOND EDITION

From the outset, *The Bottom of the Fox* was written with a follow-up edition in mind. I anticipated that people would come forward with new information, which they have, as well as point out errors, of which there have been mercifully few.

There is not one of the original 13 chapters that has not grown, some substantially, while the second edition also includes an additional chapter and three appendices.

The first edition has received an embarrassment of praise, which is especially gratifying because much of it has come from people who knew Eddie Joubert well. Others appreciated the history of the Poconos that is threaded through the book, with one long-time resident suggesting that the second edition be subtitled Welcome to the Poconos. This Is What It Could Have Been.

SHAUN D. MULLEN
September 2010

Chapter One:

WHAT THE BARRED OWL SAW

The smell of snow was in the air as Eddie Joubert opened the back door of the Bottom of the Fox and walked down the steps for the last time. It was only a few minutes after 5 on this Saturday evening in late November 1981, but except for a thin ribbon of light in the western sky it already was dark.

Eddie paused on the bottom step, pulled a battered Zippo lighter inscribed with the motto "Look for the Union Label on the Box" from the right pocket of a well worn leather vest and an unfiltered Camel cigarette from a pack in the left pocket. He had recently gotten into the habit of scanning the backyard with special care whenever he left his bar in Delaware Water Gap, a village at the eastern end of the Pocono Mountains straddling the Maine-to-Georgia Appalachian Trail.

He was a scrapper from way back, a streetsmart former trucker and Teamsters Union organizer from North Jersey who was capable of taking care of himself, but he recently had begun wondering whether he'd live to see his 47th birthday.

Eddie had found out about something awful. Worse yet, the perpetrators were aware that he was onto them. Further complicating his untidy life, someone had tried to torch a duplex two doors down Main Street from the Fox a few days earlier. His younger brother Phil, his girlfriend and their neighbor Linda Fogel and her three boys had been able to escape unharmed.

Beneath a canopy of hemlocks in the backyard were empty beer cases and other jetsam from the bar, an extension ladder, picnic table, an old multi-colored Volvo station wagon, an even older primer gray Dodge pickup truck, and the pride of the Fox fleet -- a 1954 four-door Dodge Coronet with a Gyromatic transmission and 296 horsepower Hemi engine. There was a large "Stay Out" sign nailed to the trunk of the largest of the hemlocks and a carefully piled stack of rough milled lumber awaiting future projects peeking out from behind a blue plastic tarpaulin.

Firewood for the jack stove in the kitchen was scattered everywhere. Firewood was as much a part of Eddie's life as eating and shitting. Chopping. Chain-sawing. Splitting. Loading. Hauling. Unloading. Stacking. Burning. If you wanted to stay warm during the long Pocono winters, you just did it.

Eddie could keep a woodstove cranking in his sleep. Open the damper. Open the door. Bank the coals to one side.

Shovel out the ashes from the other side. Bank the coals back over. Shovel out the rest of the ashes. Load more wood. Close the door. Wait until you hear the whoosh of the wood catching. Close the damper. Go back to bed. He had done it a thousand times.

Beyond the yard was an immense sycamore said to be the largest in Monroe County. Eddie loved the tree, and many a morning he watched the same three or four crows alight on its branches and raucously gossip before setting out on their daily rounds. On summer evenings, the tree's multi-colored bark and big lobed leaves shimmered in the setting sun. If he squinted just so, the sycamore looked like a great jeweled ship with glittering sails.

At night, a solitary barred owl held vigil on its highest branches. The barred is the most elusive of owls, and Eddie had heard its distinctive barking cry many times before he finally saw it silhouetted in a rising full moon. Its "hoo, hoo, too-HOO hoo, hoo, too-HOO aw" sounded to him like "Who cooks for you? Who cooks for you all?" and was a counterpoint to the sound of traffic below the Fox on Interstate 80 at a toll bridge over the Delaware River, the dividing line between Pennsylvania and New Jersey, and between the beauty of the Poconos and the mean streets he had left behind seven years earlier.

The Minsi Indians, who farmed, hunted and fished the area

long before white man arrived, had uses for almost everything in the verdant Pocono woodlands. But the Minsi passed sycamores by. Their corkscrew-shaped grain made the wood unsuitable for cutting and even the characteristic winged fruit lacked nutrition. Here was a tree that had no value other than its beauty, and Eddie loved that.

Eddie took a last drag on the cigarette, dropped it into a rusty can at the foot of the steps, pulled up the frayed collar of his green nylon bomber jacket and stepped out into the yard. He'd deal with the firewood after he fetched some things from the freezer in the cellar.

The Fox's cellar was not a welcoming place. Cellars seldom are, but there was an indelibly creepy feeling about this one.

Maybe it had something to do with the legend that the Fox was haunted by the spirits of long departed souls because it had been built on a Minsi burial ground. It was a good story, but didn't jibe with the fact that the Minsi, the northernmost tribe of the Lenni Lenape, interred their elders on high rock outcroppings so they would be a little closer to the heavens and not at the bottom of a hill such as where the Fox was located. No one except Indian-smart Glenn Fisher paid much notice to this small but significant detail. No one was really sure if Eddie had Indian blood either, but he spoke proudly of having a Native American heritage and had hung a plaque over the Fox's bar alluding to the Lenni Lenape that read:

> THE WOODLAND PEOPLE:
> IF YOU THINK THEY'RE GONE
> YOU'RE WRONG

Nor did Eddie's friends inquire about the mysterious trips that he and Fisher took to tribal lands in upstate New York. They wouldn't have gotten a straight answer if they had. Eddie was not inclined to wear jewelry. It could be a dangerous nuisance when using a chainsaw, but he usually wore a beaded Indian amulet set off with two bear claws that he had been gifted on one of the trips. He was wearing the necklace this evening. When asked about it he'd give the same answer: "It would lose its powers if I told you."

The Fox's regulars joked about the spirits, but there were times when even Fisher had to admit that there might be something to the burial-ground tale. The employees called them "Dead Nights."

On some days about the time that the day crowd had left and before the night crowd arrived, the bar would be empty and the half dozen or so people who lived in the rented rooms upstairs were gone. There would be an oppressive feeling of heavy air, as one bartender described it.

The bartender would hear a voice:

Get out! Get out! Get out!

She sometimes would do just that and had closed early on several evenings.

There also was joking about whether the spirits were good or evil. Fisher did have an answer for that: It depended on whether the energy of the Fox was good or evil. That view was about to be sorely tested.

The cellar stank of sewage from the Water Gap's decrepit sewer system, and the dark stone walls and earthen floor soaked up the meager light from a single light bulb. Eddie was only 5-foot-8, although his presence could be so commanding that people would swear he was much taller. Still, he had to duck to avoid walking into cobwebs dangling from between the rafters.

The cellar was entered through a door at the bottom of a ramp. Inside was a temperamental oil-fired furnace that had been converted to run on coal and a massive floor safe of unknown lineage that would not have been out of place in Wyatt Earp's office in Dodge City, a chest freezer filled with soups, steaks, hamburger patties, flounder fillets and French fries, a washer and dryer, a woodworking shop, disused kitchen equipment and a 55-gallon drum filled to overflowing with empty beer bottles.

Eddie especially hated going into the cellar at night. The awful something had spooked him so badly that he had stashed a knife near the freezer in addition to the baseball bat and rifle that he kept behind the bar. He also rigged a short length of white insulated telephone wire over the door that would be disturbed if anyone tried to open it. Eddie had told two trusted employees about the wire but not the reason for it. They were to let him know right away if it was out of place.

Although it was obvious to Eddie's daughter Cheryl and his closest friends that he was in fear of his life, he hadn't confided about the awful something to anyone except his dear friend Rosalie and two other women.

Rosalie was Rosalie Sorrels, a folk singer whom one critic has called "the hillbilly Edith Piaf" for her eclectic vocal stylings. Sorrels had met Eddie while playing at a club in New Hope down the Delaware River near Philadelphia. He invited her back to the Fox, and although the Poconos were out of her way there was something so charming about him that she agreed before she knew what she was doing. They stayed up all night drinking and telling stories, and as they watched the sun rise over the sycamore she knew that this was a place where she could get back in touch with her inner gypsy.

Sorrels fell in love with Eddie and the scene around the Fox. There was an unpretentiousness about him and his friends that she craved. Several were Vietnam veterans who were seriously into alcohol, marijuana, trips and anything else that would help them deal with – or blot out – their memories. Having been deeply scarred by a few wars of her own, Sorrels could relate.

Eddie and his friends loved Sorrels right back. She would have a big pot of jambalaya cooking for the jazz musicians who would stop by late at night for jam sessions after playing local clubs or the resorts that were the backbone of Poconos tourism. Attracted by the low home prices, several musicians had moved to the Gap and nearby communities and also would drop in after they played at clubs in New York City, a 70 mile drive out Interstate 80.

Sorrels' youngest son had just been paroled from a Colorado penitentiary and would be arriving in the Poconos on the Saturday after Thanksgiving. Although Eddie had his hands full with one of his own sons, Sorrels thought that he might be able to talk some sense into hers.

Earlier in the week Sorrels had asked Eddie to drive her to Saratoga in upstate New York for Thanksgiving dinner with friends, including William Kennedy, who was working on the last book in his acclaimed Albany trilogy. Sorrels was sure that Eddie and the writer would hit it off, but Eddie hated holidays because they were when real families got together and his family seemed to be anything but. St. Patrick's Day was the only exception because it was an excuse to let loose. He told Sorrels that he would think about it. But he never got back to her and she was unable to shake the feeling that something was very wrong as she hit the road on Thanksgiving morning.

Eddie briefly came out of his funk the next morning, a Friday. With the first snow of the season on the way, he and Fisher decided to drive to Woodstock in upstate New York to cut firewood for a woman friend.

If they weren't cutting firewood for themselves, Eddie and Fisher were cutting firewood for others. It sometimes was an adventure, like the time Eddie had driven through a blizzard to deliver wood and food to a woman and her children. Just south of Woodstock, they came upon a state police roadblock. The Volvo wagon reeked because they had just smoked a joint of Fisher's potent homegrown marijuana, and the car stood out like a psychedelic rock poster on wheels, but they were waved through.

After cutting and stacking a cord or so of firewood, they had stayed up most of the night drinking. Eddie wanted to go back out to the woodlot to work off his hangover, but he had to get back to the Gap. Linda Fogel was getting married on Saturday afternoon. She had been a waitress at the Fox and her wedding was the social event of the season, a rare occasion when Gap outsiders and insiders mingled and could pretend how well that they got along. He didn't much care for the guy Fogel was marrying and he definitely didn't care for weddings, his own being the most bittersweet of memories. Besides which, he had to work Saturday night because bartender-manager Kate Holmes, who had made Fogel's bridal dress, would be off.

Holmes had taped a note to the kitchen refrigerator for Eddie with phone messages, a list of who was supposed to be paid that night and what he needed to bring up from the cellar freezer. Among the messages was one from Sorrels, who had called to remind him that she and her son would be coming over after she got back from Saratoga.

Late in the afternoon, several people stopped by the Fox on their way to the wedding reception. Eddie smoked a joint with some of them and snorted a line of cocaine when offered some. He still felt a trace of a hangover as he descended the cellar ramp to fetch whatever Holmes had told him to bring up from the freezer.

He paused at the cellar door. Damn. He'd forgotten the list and started to turn around when he reflexively glanced at the top of the door. The wire wasn't there. He looked closer. The wire still wasn't there.

The wire has to be there!, said a voice in his head.

His heart suddenly was racing. He went up on tiptoes, but only about halfway on the first try because his old work boots weren't used to being stretched that way. He went up further on the second try. Still no wire.

Where's the fucking wire?

His heart was now beating so hard that it felt like it was going to explode out of his chest.

Where's the fucking wire? Sweet mother of Jesus! It's happening!

Damned hangover.

Work, brain, work! Un-fucking-believable! Where's the wire?

As he again looked for the wire in the dim light cast by a floodlight on the back wall of the Fox he realized that he was not alone. There was someone behind him and he sensed that someone else was lurking behind the cellar door.

It's happening!

He started to turn but was knocked against the cellar wall by a sharp blow to the head.

Ouch! No! Hurt! It's happening! No hurt no!

He tried to fight back. There was a shovel at the top of the ramp, but it was too far away. The sheathed knife on his belt was under several layers of clothing and he couldn't get to the knife in the cellar. The ramp was too narrow for him to slip past his attacker and too far below the yard to try to scramble up and out. There was no way to escape.

Trapped! It's happening! Hurt! Hurt Hurt!

Now he heard a second voice in his head.

Get out! Get out! Get out!

He continued to turn.

The second voice called out again:

Get out! Get out! Get out!

Then his own voice:

Hot. Thirsty. Ouch! Get pipe! Hot. Thirsty. Pipe! Can't get out!

He had spotted a length of PVC pipe leaning against the cellar wall, but it too was out of reach. As he turned a little more his legs gave out and he began falling backwards. His right knee hit the wall. He tried to pull himself up with his right hand but all he could do was grab a fistful of dirt and hemlock needles.

Hold on. Got to hold on! Get up. Hot. So thirsty. Can't get out!

It felt like it was taking forever to fall. He threw his left arm over his head in another attempt to pull himself up and grabbed more dirt and needles as he finally landed on his back. His skull smashed into the ground, the voices in his head now barely audible.

Hot. Thirsty. Sweet Jesus! It's happening! Dear God! Please! No! No! No! Please! Ple---, whispered the first voice.

Get out! Get ou-. Ge ---, whispered the second.

The attacker stood over Eddie gasping for air as he clenched an ax over his head with both hands. The business end twinkled every so slightly in the dim glow of the floodlight as it hurtled down into the center of Eddie's forehead. The attacker raised the ax again. It came down again, cutting deeper. Then a third time, nearly amputating his left hand at the wrist. And a fourth time, slicing through his jeans and into his thigh above the left knee.

The attacker peered down at him, the ax now at his side. His breathing became more measured. The only sounds were the blood gurgling from Eddie's head and the thrum of traffic from down on the interstate.

A car door slammed. The attacker looked up, oblivious to the blood splattered over his face and body. He seemed reluctant to leave. Another car door slammed and there were voices. The attacker looked up again, sighed deeply, took another long look at Eddie, hoisted the ax over his shoulder and wearily walked up the ramp and disappeared into the darkness.

The barred owl peered down from the sycamore.

"Hoo, hoo, too-HOO hoo, hoo, too-HOO," it cried. "Hoo, hoo, too-HOO hoo, hoo, too-HOO aw."

Chapter Two:

OF LENAPES AND LAND GRABS

The biggest lie told about the Pocono Mountains is that they are mountains. While that technically is true, they aren't mountains in the sense that the Colorado Rockies or Swiss Alps are mountains. The Poconos are more like worn down nubs, the result of a geologic bump and grind that began 900 million years ago and continues to this day.

It was during the Precambrian Era that this dance began. The continents collided, creating an immense supercontinent and the first Appalachian mountain range. Almost as quickly – in geologic time, at least – the supercontinent split apart and the Appalachians washed into a primordial sea, the ancestor of the Atlantic Ocean. The continents reversed course and began moving back together about 500 million years ago during the Ordovician Period. As they crept closer, sediment from the first mountains was pushed back out of the sea, forming a second Appalachian range. The continents again collided, resulting in a second supercontinent that geologists call Pangaea. The new Appalachians were pushed westward as the dance continued, forming the parallel ridges that are so evident when you look at a relief map of the Poconos.

About 200 million years ago, the beginning of the Jurassic Period, Pangaea began breaking up and the resulting continents drifted toward the present-day positions of North America, Europe and Africa. Then the Appalachians began to shrink yet again because of erosion from wind and water, and most notably because of ice as the Earth went through a period of profound cooling. This ice, over a mile thick in some places, carved out valleys, lakes and rivers, including the mighty Delaware, as well as rounded off the modern-day Appalachians, which are known in Pennsylvania as the Alleghenys, to the north as the Adirondacks, Berkshires, Taconics, Greens, Whites, Longfellows and Notre Dames, and to the south as the Blue Ridges, Great Smokys and Cumberlands. The 2,173-mile-long Appalachian Trail, which was completed in 1937, runs atop a ridgeline from Mt. Katahdin at the border with Canada to northern Georgia, bisecting the village where the Fox was located.

The mountains that define the eastern edge of the Poconos are as worn down as any in the Appalachians. The Kittatinnys have a uniformly flat (some would say boring) ridgeline broken in only one place by a spectacular mile-wide gap where layers of limestone, quartz and shale are laid bare and plunge 1,300 feet from the ridgeline at an almost precise 45-degree angle to the Delaware River before reappearing in mirror image on the other side. This is the Delaware Water Gap.

The first humans didn't arrive in the Poconos until the last glaciers had receded and the transition from tundra to forest was well underway. It was the onset of the Holocene Period, the name given to the most recent 11,000 years of the Earth's history. The Minsi, Shawnee and Paupack tribes, the first permanent settlers of any consequence, arrived 800 years ago – about the time that the barons of the Runnymeade were demanding that King John sign the Magna Carta.

The Minsi named the river that ran through the gap in the mountains the Lenape and the wide valley above the gap the Minisink. The Minsi were farmers, fishermen, hunters, toolmakers and carvers. They grew corn and tobacco in soil made fertile by river flooding. They fished for eel, sturgeon and shad in the river, trout in its many tributaries and speared sunfish in a pond in a meadow atop the Kittatinny ridgeline. They hunted deer, bear, turkey, mink and beaver in the woodlands. They made arrowheads, spear points and adzes from flint and chert and cooking vessels from soapstone cut from faraway quarries connected by an extensive network of footpaths. They bore and raised their young in the valley and, as Glenn Fisher knew, buried their dead on the highest rock outcroppings so that they would be just a little bit closer to their heavenly forebears. Life was good.

The beginning of the end of that good life came on August

28, 1609 when the Dutch ship Half Moon, captained by Henry Hudson, arrived on the shores of the New World and he founded New Amsterdam. Change had played out in the Poconos in increments of millions of years, but soon was occurring at a speed and in ways that the Minsi were unable to comprehend, let alone slow down. Within 25 years of Hudson's arrival, Dutch colonist Hendrick Van Allen had trekked to the gap in the mountains and opened a copper mine. Copper ore was soon being transported by mule-drawn wagons to smelteries nearly 100 miles away in what became New York state on Copper Mine Road, which was built along the New Jersey side of the river on an Indian footpath. It was the first road of any length in the New World.

The Minsi traded pelts, tobacco and foodstuffs to the Dutch for iron pots, needles and cloth. This commerce flourished, but in 1664 the British took over New Amsterdam, which the Dutch had famously purchased from a local tribe for $24 worth of beads.

The Dutch were sent packing and Van Allen was ordered to close his mine and sail home. Local legend has it that he had fallen in love with the comely Winona, an expert canoeist and archer and daughter of Chief Wissinoming. When he tearfully told Winona that he was leaving her behind, the Minsi princess jumped to her death from an outcropping high above the gap in the mountains. Van Allen followed.

As the British were wont to do as they went a conquering, they renamed everything in their path. The river and tribe became the Delaware for Lord De La Warr, otherwise known as Sir Thomas West, and the gap in the mountains became Delaware Water Gap. New Amsterdam, of course, became New York City. The closest person to a white chief for the Minsi was William Penn, a devout Quaker, crusader for religious freedom and founder of Philadelphia in 1682, who was into King Charles II for a heap of crown sterling. Years of war with France had left the royal treasury empty, so Charles paid off Penn with a proverbial king's ransom in the form of an enormous tract of land between Maryland and New York, much of it woodland, that was larger than all of England.

Penn, like Eddie, admired the Minsi for their intelligence, intimate relationship with their surroundings and willingness to mediate rather than fight when problems arose.

The tribe seemed to fit perfectly into Penn's Quaker-based "Holy Experiment" -- that whites and Indians could live together in peace. To that end the colonial proprietor in chief entered into a treaty in 1701 with the Lenni Lenape nation, of which the Minsi were a part. The Indians would coexist with the English "as long as the sun will shine and the rivers flow with water." The Lenape would keep northeastern Pennsylvania, while the English would stay to the south and east along the banks of the lower Delaware and Schuylkill rivers.

But like other early colonial leaders to the north in New York and New England and to the south in Virginia, Penn lost control of his realm. As the 18th century dawned, the settler population was growing quickly and expanding outward into Indian lands. Then Iroquois raiding parties began moving through the colony, claiming the Susquehanna Valley by right of conquest, which included the right to sell the lands of the indigenous tribes back to those very tribes.

As far as the Lenape were concerned, Penn was the last white leader who kept his word. His son, Thomas Penn, and secretary, James Logan, did not share his pacifistic principals and cast their lot with the powerful Iroquois, knowing that their support was essential if the colony was to prosper.

The Lenape were bitterly alienated by the growing alliance with the Iroquois, as well as Thomas Penn's infamous Walking Treaty of 1736, which surreptitiously expropriated most of the Leanpe's ancestral lands

The usually peaceful Minsi, realizing the extent to which they had been duped, went on scalping sprees that continued through the French and Indian War in the 1760s and intermittently into the 1780s. The tribe, decimated and exhausted, finally conceded that they would never again regain their verdant valley by the river and trekked west into a region the French called the *Pays d'en Haut*, literally "the up country," where they settled in exile in multi-ethnic villages before settlers forced them further west again.

Once the Indians were disposed of, it was the dramatic beauty of the gap in the mountains that determined the future of the Poconos.

In 1793, Antoine Dutot, a French plantation owner from Santo Domingo, laid out the village of Delaware Water Gap. An inn opened in 1799 on the first road cut through the gap – a 130-mile-long stage road linking Scranton to the northwest and Philadelphia to the southeast that today is Pennsylvania Route 611 and the Gap's Main Street. Travelers began vacationing there, as did artists who portrayed the idyllic spot where the river flowed between the mountains in watercolors and oils.

Paintings of the Delaware Water Gap looked down from flocked wallpaper walls on the sofas, étagères and pianos of many a parlor of the era. The Kittatinny House, the first resort hotel, was an immediate success when it opened in

1833 a stone's throw from the eventual site of the Fox.

In 1855, rails were laid on a stage road on the Pennsylvania side of the Delaware Water Gap and more and more people, many from well-heeled New York and Philadelphia families, arrived by train to take the bracing mountain air. In modern parlance, the Poconos were hot. But an increasing number of visitors were now drawn to resorts where there were activities other than sitting on one's backside. These included the Buck Hill Inn in Barrett Township, which is considered by some people to be the first modern resort in America, and the Buckwood Inn in Shawnee. One by one, the Gap resorts closed and in 1931 the Kittatinny House burned to the ground.

With the opening of man-made Lake Wallenpaupack and its 52 miles of shoreline in 1926, the resort industry could boast of an impressive range of family-friendly attractions in addition to lush forests and sparkling mountain streams. And family friendly they were. Card playing and games of chance were prohibited and golf and other sports were not permitted on Sundays. Although the resorts would let down their hair a bit in later years, the conservative streak that has long characterized the region meant certain defeat for initiatives to legalize casino gambling and other perceived vices. Even after limited casino gambling was narrowly approved in a local initiative in 2006, the Poconos would never be confused with Atlantic City, let alone Las

Vegas.

By the end of World War II, the resort industry was selling the Poconos as the "Honeymoon Capital of the World," attracting returning GIs and their brides by the thousands.

The first commercial ski area opened in 1946 and artificial snowmaking began in 1950, although no innovation burnished the region's image more than the heart-shaped bathtub, first introduced at Cove Haven resort in 1963. Celebrities flocked to the Poconos. Golfing great Arnold Palmer and comedian Jackie Gleason were regulars at the renamed Buckwood, now called the Shawnee Inn. President Eisenhower stopped by to play golf. Even if its mountains were more nub-like than lofty, the Poconos had become a major attraction.

But behind the bright lights of the ski lodges and honeymoon cottages there was – and still is – an appalling level of poverty and wide gulf between the haves and have nots, some of whom are resort workers who are paid meager wages with little chance of advancement. Stroudsburg, the largest municipality in the Poconos and often the first stop on long-distance bus routes from New York City to the west, has long been a jumping off point for abused women and other people trying to escape the degradations of the urban existence.

There also was one of the least noticed and most neglected minority groups in the United States – the mountain people who settled so far back in the hills that Poconos residents hardly knew they existed.

These people were the detritus of a brief logging boom in the late 19th century. While most of the loggers moved on to western Pennsylvania, Ohio and elsewhere, the weaker ones, many of them social misfits and some mentally retarded, stayed behind, the second-growth forests sheltering them and the abundant wildlife feeding their common-law wives and children, few of whom attended school or could read and write.

Except for small pockets, the mountain people are long gone today. The dirt tracks they walked became wagon roads and then paved highways as the resorts and other development spread from Stroudsburg and East Stroudsburg, impinging on and finally destroying their hovels. Truant officers, revenue agents and public-health officials did what development couldn't. Most mountain people were absorbed into society. They got jobs. Their children went to school. But their legacy lives on as a metaphor for the grinding poverty that exists in the Poconos to this day.

Several events were to change the Poconos forever, but

none was as dramatic as the completion of Interstate 80 in 1971.

I-80, the longest of the interstate highways, originally was to bypass Stroudsburg and East Stroudsburg well to the south, but city fathers insisted that it run through the heart of their communities, a decision that was so shortsighted that it prompted one old-time politician to declare that the four lanes of concrete were a "gigantic sewer pipe" on the day that the ribbon was cut to mark its opening. Practically overnight, the dynamic of the region was transformed -- and not for the better. About half of the tourists arrived in the Poconos on Delaware, Lackawanna and Hudson trains that stopped at a necklace of stations near Fernwood, Buck Hill, Mount Airy, Pocono Manor and other resorts, but the DL&H was unable to compete with the interstate and passenger service soon went under.

"The sense of adventure that the Poconos offered, the feeling that you were going to someplace special was destroyed," said one longtime resident who worked at resorts before and after I-80 opened. "The very concept of the resort was destroyed. We became just another place to get off the highway between New York City and California."

A Gap resident says that the village changed practically overnight.

"People used to leave their keys in their ignitions and even their wallets on their dashboards," he said. "Then all of a sudden there was crime because of the interstate. Mostly petty crime, mind you, but the feeling of safety and insularity was lost forever."

Resorts began to close. Run by the third and fourth generations of the same families, the owners did not have the resources, deep pockets and imagination to compete with newer and flashier destinations like Disney World, Las Vegas and the Bahamas, all of which took a page from the Poconos' own play book and sold themselves as family-friendly resorts.

The demand that I-80 be routed through the heart of the Stroudsburgs was anything but typical. These cities are, in fact, the only ones that the interstate bisects between Paterson, New Jersey and Salt Lake City, Utah.

Today traffic accidents on I-80 occur with numbing regularity, resulting in severe congestion on streets and byways from the spillover of traffic. Even the smallest incident can bring the Stroudsburgs to a halt. Because of its footprint, the highway and its harrowing exit and entrance ramps can't be enlarged to handle traffic levels far greater than it was engineered for, and today the commute between the Poconos and New York City is considered to be the worst in the nation.

Then a bitter war erupted over a plan to dam the Delaware River three miles above the I-80 bridge at Tocks Island, creating an immense reservoir that would submerge hundreds of homes and farms. This conflict exposed a deep animosity toward outsiders and eventually would shake the Gap from its decades-long lethargy just as Eddie was settling into the business of running the Fox.

Next came an explosion of time shares, a marketing innovation in which people shared ownership of townhouses in the developments that became ubiquitous as the family resorts faded. People using time shares tended to stay in at night, and combined with resort closings destroyed many of the music clubs, putting musicians out of work.

Finally, lured by billboards and television ads that touted the Poconos as a green and safe world that could not be more different than the Bronx, thousands of families traveled out the interstate and bought their first homes.

"Why rent?" read a typical ad. "Our goal is homeownership for you and your family. Every American wants it; every American deserves it."

For many of these families, things did not work out well.

While some soon found that the five-hour daily grind to and from their jobs in the city was a marriage killer, many more fell victim to a land-rush culture in which shady developers and predatory mortgage companies and banks, often working in tandem, took advantage of lax regulation and enabling local politicians to target middle-class blacks and Hispanics. The result was a housing bubble that was impossible to sustain and burst long before the market collapsed nationally.

Many of the new homes were of shoddy construction and built on the sensitive wetlands and bogs that were part of what made the Poconos special, while by 2004, one in five mortgaged homes in Monroe County was in foreclosure. The situation has only gotten worse as struggling homeowners have failed to stay a step ahead of the sheriff.

The Poconos had indeed seemed a million miles from civilization, as Eddie once put it, but today it is much too similar to the very places and the problems that he had wanted to escape.

Chapter Three:

THE HIKER

It was back in August of 1977 when the lone hiker crossed the meadow at Sunfish Pond on the Appalachian Trail and began the steep descent to the Gap. After stopping for a few minutes to shelter from the late afternoon heat and drain his canteen, the hiker hoisted his pack onto his shoulders with a practiced weariness, adjusted his sweat-soaked bush hat and continued on, mess kit clanking against his bedroll in a tinny imitation of a cowbell.

No one would mistake Owen Owen for a cow. A scarecrow perhaps. The torso and head of the 23-year-old Irishman seemed to disappear under his ripstop nylon burden and from a distance he looked like a big red backpack atop a pair of spindly legs that disappeared into gartered knee socks and outsized boots. Some of the hikers with whom he shared campfires in the evening teased him about his ear-to-ear freckles, incessant use of the British expression "Bob's your uncle" and big blister covered feet, but he would disarm them with an infectious smile and a brogue that he had pretty much lost over the years at English boarding schools and Cambridge University, but summoned and slathered on when there was an attractive young woman to hear his story.

That story invariably was a hit for the earnest hikers that he encountered, most of whom had never ventured more than a few hundred miles from home and had a romantically gauzy view of the British Isles.

His father and namesake, Owen Owen would explain, was the chief solicitor for a Dublin brewery who had expected his eldest son to follow him into the profession. But this only child was not ready to settle down. He had announced with great solemnity that he was going to the States -- alone -- to indulge his passion for hiking and would walk the Appalachian Trail from north to south and then back again for good measure. He was soon flying into Boston after breaking off his engagement to a longtime sweetheart whose own father was a duke and lived in a manor house straight out of a Bram Stoker novel. He turned aside her pleas that there were perfectly good trails to hike close to home as well as his father's threats to disown him because Owenses were not vagabonds.

The story was more or less true, although there were a few embellishments: His not-to-be future father-in-law actually was a mere viscount, while the longest hike he had ever taken was when his car broke down out in the Gog Magog Hills during his last year at university and he had to walk a few miles to the nearest garage. No one was more surprised than Owen Owen himself when he trooped out of an Eastern Mountain Sports store in Boston outfitted in hiker's mufti and hitchhiked to Rutland, Vermont, where he had decided to meet the Appalachian Trail for no reason other than he liked the sound of the city's name.

He had celebrated his last night in civilization with a steak dinner and a showing of *Star Wars*, the huge hit movie of that summer, before picking up the trail. His spirits had not always matched the sunny skies during the first two weeks, and on this afternoon he was especially homesick despite the camaraderie of other hikers. He felt overwhelmed by the goal he had set for himself as he tried to settle back into an ambling, arm-swinging gait that an experienced hiker had tutored him on while pointing out that the pricey Raichle boots that he had bought at EMS were suitable only for experienced hikers and raising blisters on those who weren't.

The Kittatinny ridge soon broke away to Owen Owen's left and he caught glimpses of the languid Delaware River through the woods to his right. The waters looked inviting as canoers and rafters floated downstream. He broke through the trees to an overlook above the Interstate 80 toll bridge and the Gap.

While no one would confuse the village of Delaware Water Gap with St. Nicholas Gate in Dublin or the Delaware with the River Liffey, it was a welcome sight. There would be no trying to seduce a lass by the light of a campfire this evening. Owen Owen knew that a few brews (ice cold as the Yanks drank them) to damp down the trail dust, a good meal and a hot shower (even if it meant reneging on his determination to never get a hotel room) would be good for what ailed him. He had been loath to smoke marijuana out on the trail, and perhaps he could find someone with whom to share a bowl from the bag he had bought from a hippie in Rutland.

He followed the trail markers down to Deerfield Creek, then under the interstate and to the pedestrian walkway on the eastbound side of the toll bridge. Now in Pennsylvania, the markers led to a rise and he was soon on the Gap's Main Street. On the other side of the street was a place called the Deer Head Inn. He turned right and strode past the Presbyterian Church of the Mountain, which reminded him of the church in the village that one of his father's servants built on his electric train layout when he was a child. At the bottom of the hill was a welcoming sight.

The Irishman's first impression of the Fox would occupy a special place in his pantheon of world-traveling stories, and he retold it endlessly over the years: How he felt like Luke Skywalker entering the crazy bar filled with space aliens on the planet Alderaan in Star Wars. His second impression was that the characters around the Fox's bar indeed seemed to be from a galaxy far, far away.

Owen Owen not only found someone with whom to share a bowl, but he and the bar's owner, an affable man by the name of Eddie, the gnome-like Glenn Fisher and Bill Reinhart smoked their way through most of his bag during the extended after-hours lucubrations that he soon found were part of the Fox's charm.

Reinhart had done one tour in Vietnam as an infantryman, lived in the Haight-Ashbury district of San Francisco at the height of the Flower Power movement, then went to flight school and a second tour in Vietnam as a helicopter pilot.

None of the men seemed impressed with the Irishman's forsaken sweetheart story. They teased him about his brogue and could care less about dukes and duchesses. He certainly could offer nothing from his comparatively brief and boring existence that could match the tales they told, especially Reinhart's exploits in the Haight and Vietnam and the lore of the mountains and river that seemed so central to their lives. He stayed the night, the next day and then another, soon feeling not like a newcomer but just another member of a big, unruly family that considered the Fox their living room and wouldn't get scolded for putting their feet on the furniture. A band called Asparagus Sun-

shine played one evening and Fisher teased him into dancing a jig. When a pretty young woman took his arm, the band was drowned out by claps, cries and hoots. He had company that night in one of the rooms upstairs.
On his last full day in the Gap, Fisher took him into Stroudsburg where he bought a more suitable pair of boots at Dunkleberger's and then drove him out River Road along the other side of the Delaware from the Appalachian Trail for a tour of some of Fisher's old haunts when he had led the Tocks Island squatters against the Corps of Engineers. They picked lady slipper orchids to bring back to one of the bartenders and watercress to garnish sandwiches for the resumption of Owen Owen's southbound trek.

There was to be a going-away party for Owen Owen that night. Another excuse for a party. But the Happy Hour crowd was strangely subdued when they got back to the Fox.

"There's been a murder," Eddie explained. "They found a guy's body in the back of his car this morning down the road at the Arrow Island Overlook. A marijuana dealer. They say that he was strangled and beaten up something awful."

Owen Owen suddenly felt relieved that all his pot had been smoked. He asked if it was too dangerous for him to resume his hike.

"You'll be fine," Fisher assured him. "He was killed well off the trail."

"You can be sure that the police will be all over it," someone else said.

Owen Owen asked if anyone knew the victim. A bartender allowed that the young man had been in the Fox a few times in recent weeks and noted that since press reports said he had just turned 21, he had been underage. Eddie didn't recall him. At least not at first.

No matter, because the murder of David Allen Gross would come back to haunt Eddie and shake the Gap to its core.

Chapter Four:

DOWN BY THE RIVER

For all the fury that it unleashed, Tocks Island isn't much to look at -- a negligible spit of sand covered with a few oaks and sycamores and some scrub brush that sits midstream in the Delaware River about three miles above the Water Gap.

The bitter war over the Army Corps of Engineers plan to dam the river at Tocks, creating an immense reservoir that would submerge hundreds of homes and farms, would be a lightning rod for the nascent American environmental movement. It would destroy the careers of politicians, be the cause of suicides, arsons and violence, and expose deep tears in the social fabric of the Poconos. The war unleashed a bitterness against outsiders and the dam's powerful, politically connected backers that seems just as intense today, while it set in motion events that would bring together Eddie, Glenn Fisher and many of the other people who would shake the Gap from its lethargy.

The idea of taming the Delaware had been a twinkle in the eye of entrepreneurs since before the Revolutionary War. In the 1770s, the first man-made changes were made to the river when a channel was cut through the rapids at Trenton, New Jersey to facilitate the passage of coal barges. It seemed inevitable that the river would be dammed, but in 1783 Pennsylvania and New Jersey bowed to pressure from powerful sawmill owners, whose barges needed an unobstructed river, and signed an anti-dam treaty.

The treaty was challenged repeatedly as the Industrial Revolution spread from England to the young nation, and factories and mills proliferated downriver from the Poconos. In an 1852 decision that complicated an already contentious issue, the U.S. Supreme Court ruled that textile mill owners could not raise interstate issues like damming a river that flowed through several states unless one of the states did so first. In 1890, industrialist Charles C. Worthington bought 6,500 acres of land abutting the New Jersey side of the river above the Water Gap that included Sunfish Pond where the Minsi had fished and Owen Owen had hiked by. Not coincidentally, the New Jersey legislature soon enacted a law allowing the creation of companies to build hydroelectric dams. In 1913, one such dam was proposed at Belvidere, 15 miles downriver from the Water Gap, and in 1918 six dams were proposed as part of a massive Boston-to-Washington hydroelectric system, but the treaty still held.

New York City's unquenchable thirst for water would break the deadlock. In 1931, as the Great Depression spread, the

U.S. Supreme Court affirmed New York's right to divert water from the Delaware based on the principle of equitable apportionment; that is, each state in the river basin had the right to a fair share of its water.

Three developments in the mid-1930s would frame future debate over the fate of the last major free-flowing river east of the Mississippi: The Army Corps of Engineers recommended that a dam be built at Tocks, the Tennessee Valley Authority was formed, and a study by the city of Philadelphia concluded that the Tocks site was unsuitable.

Under the Corps' plan, a huge reinforced concrete dam would be built, but the proposal was shelved because money for such an ambitious project was not available during those lean times.

The Tennessee Valley Authority, a cornerstone of President Roosevelt's New Deal, gave the Corps unprecedented authority to build dams and hydroelectric plants in Tennessee, Kentucky, Alabama and Mississippi. The TVA may have been a godsend in the rural South where electricity still had not reached many farms and smaller communities, but was viewed as a federal power grab by politicians in the Delaware River basin. They were determined to not allow Washington to control what happened to *their* river.

Philadelphia's water needs also were growing. As the Depression receded the city expressed interest in reviving the Corps' Tocks plan, but its own study of the site concluded that there were big problems.

First was the violence that would be done to the surrounding area by a reservoir. Second was the impact on recreation. Third was the need for elaborate and expensive filtration and chemical treatment plants because of the buildup of algae in a reservoir. Fourth and most importantly, there were questions about whether the riverbed could support a concrete dam, and the Corps itself was to ascertain in its own 1942 study that where there was thought to be bedrock beneath the river there instead were remnants of the last Ice Age -- an unstable mix of glacial till, drift and alluvial deposits.

The study did get one thing wrong: It asserted that a dam would control flooding.

As Princess Winona and her Minsi brothers well knew, the most severe flooding occurs on tributaries where high waters breach banks much more quickly than on the Delaware. Dam or not, tributaries and not the river itself are where the most damage occurs, something that was borne out in horrifying fashion in August 1955 when hurricanes Connie and Diane ravaged the Poconos, dumping 20 inches of rain in less than a week. Some 78 people perished, most of them from flood surges that turned babbling brooks into raging torrents. The surge on usually docile Brodhead Creek crested at 30 feet, destroying a church camp and sweeping 38 people to their deaths, most of them children huddled on the top floor of the main building.

Advocates of a Tocks dam saw an opening and drove right through it. While the 1942 study had concluded that a concrete dam would not be feasible, the Corps now asserted that the absence of bedrock could be addressed by an earth and rock-fill dam with a greatly decreased slope to distribute its weight over a larger area.

The hurricanes also marked the end of resistance by the states to federal involvement. In 1959, support for the dam took a giant leap with creation of the Delaware River Basin Commission, comprised of the governors of the four states in the river basin and a non-voting member from the federal government. Washington would put up the money and the Corps would oversee construction, but unlike the TVA the states would have substantial control.

In 1962, Congress authorized the appropriation of $122 million (some $860 million in today's dollars) to build an earth and rock-fill dam at Tocks, submerging the Minisink Valley and creating a 37-mile-long, 140-foot deep reservoir extending nearly to Port Jervis in upstate New York. Surrounding this monstrosity would be a 72,000-acre, 80-square-mile park to be called Delaware Water Gap National Recreation Area.

The first battle lines were drawn not over Tocks, but Sunfish Pond.

In 1965, Fisher and Casey Kays, a Hackettstown, New Jersey outdoorsman, independently began calling attention to the imminent destruction of the pond and the lovely meadow around it. With little public notice, a consortium of power companies had bought the meadow and pond and the land down to the river from the state of New Jersey for construction of a pumped-water storage system.

Fisher was a Rhodes Scholar and had been a U.S. Department of Agriculture agronomist who did environmental impact studies long before anyone knew what they were. He had a deep knowledge of native plant species and came to know Poconos flora perhaps better than anyone.

He was a harvester, not a gardener, and would clandestinely dig up specimens of rare and endangered species and propagate them in areas well off the beaten track in an effort to increase their numbers. He gifted friends and strangers alike with cuttings of butterfly bush, rose of sharon and other species, tapped maple trees for their syrup, knew the secret of how to harvest the fruit of the persimmon tree and when spicewood was at its best for drinking as a tea. He was a not bad cook, knew where the watercress ponds were and made a delicious watercress and potato soup.

Fisher stood about 5-foot-5-inches tall, had a spavined walk that made him seem even shorter, was a lousy driver and had a fondness for cryptograms and Ballantine ale, which the Minisink Hotel on River Road would keep in stock in return for his services as a handyman. He harvested and sold Christmas trees, and would look in on the elderly and infirm in times of extreme heat and cold. His idea of a good time would be to roll a fat marijuana cigarette and go for a long walk in the woods. He was painfully shy when sober, only slightly less so when he had a buzz on, and would pause to stroke his chin before responding to a comment or question, or to quote his idol, poet-naturalist Henry David Thoreau. "Man away from nature becomes unnatural" was a favorite.

His outsized views frequently got him into trouble like the time the USDA had sent him to Cuba to advise Fidel Castro's agriculture ministry before the U.S. turned against the Communist regime. Fisher liked what he saw and ended up cutting sugar cane for Castro instead of returning home when his assignment was completed, infuriating his bosses in Washington.

In 1967, Fisher and Kays joined forced with Nancy Shukaitis, a Poconos activist, to form the Lenni Lenape League. Catching the first wave of the environmental movement, they and Supreme Court Justice William O. Douglas and his young wife led a 1,000-person protest hike to Sunfish Pond. Sensitive to the negative publicity, the power companies soon sold the land back to the state.

That same year the Corps of Engineers made the first move to force out 206 families living in homes and on farms in the footprint of the reservoir in three Pennsylvania and two New Jersey counties.

Created in 1799, the Corps has a long and checkered history as the custodian of America's rivers, harbors and wetlands. As was the case with Tocks, it often has been a broker for powerful political and private interests. As was the case with Tocks, it manipulated its own engineering and economic analyses to suit its needs. And as was the case with Tocks, its tactics could be thuggish.

The Corps offered only pennies on the dollar and strong-armed residents who resisted moving out or did not want to sell on the Corps' terms with threats to bring in bulldozers. Although it would be years before the dam could be built, beginning in 1967 and continuing for five years, one family after another was forced out.

The plight of farmers left with fields to work but no farmhouses or barns was particularly poignant. The forebears of Shukaitis' father-in-law, Blanchard Michael, had arrived from England in the late 1780s during the last throes of the Minsi rebellion and had farmed the valley for six generations when the Corps announced that it was appropriating his property.

"My father-in-law lived in the belief that the farm wouldn't be taken," Shukaitis said. "I never understood how deeply he felt until he testified in federal court." Asked what the loss of his farm meant to him by a lawyer for the anti-dam coalition, the proud man burst into tears and wept inconsolably before finally summoning a response.

"I can't pass it on to my sons," he said.

As the evictions accelerated, the Corps added insult to injury, placing "Houses for Rent" ads in the *Village Voice* and other New York City newspapers. Under pressure to cut costs, it calculated that revenue could be generated by renting out now-vacant properties until the dam was completed and the reservoir began filling up.

It was an incredibly stupid move.

The ads were answered by a ragtag assortment of hippies, artists, back-to-nature freaks and squatters. They referred to themselves as River People, which was an enormous insult to the River Rats, as the people who lived in the Minisink had long called themselves.

These newcomers were soon at war with locals who were furious over the evictions, let alone the long-haired newcomers who swam nude in the river, grew marijuana between rows of corn, flirted with their daughters, and got welfare instead of working. The pro-dam *Pocono Record* cited the perorations of a Corps official: "There is not one among the squatters I would completely trust to react in what would be considered a normal, lucid manner," and asserted that there was widespread lawlessness, drug use and venereal disease.

In 1971, the Pappalardos were the last family to leave the valley. The Corps had appraised their lovely three-bedroom fieldstone house and 20 acres for a measly $16,000.

Unlike the Michael family, the Pappalardos were relative newcomers.

Anthony Pappalardo, the oldest of six sons of Italian immigrants, moved into the Minisink in 1940 and started a chicken farm. Eggs were rationed during World War II and he prospered by selling them in New York City.

"We felt like Native Americans. It was a blatant theft of

our land," son Pete Pappalardo said. "We had to move to a house trailer. My mother put up a sign on it that said 'Halfway House'. My brother Freddie peeled away the 'W' and the 'Y' so the sign read "Half a House."

Beyond the bad publicity, the cost of the project was spiraling out of control and had doubled to $240 million ($1.2 billion in today's dollars) at a time when the Vietnam War had sucked dry the federal treasury.

The second wave of environmentalism came, of all places, from the Nixon administration. On New Years Day 1970, four months before the first Earth Day, a president not remembered for his environmental accomplishments signed the National Environmental Policy Act, which required that extensive studies be carried out on how federal projects like Tocks would affect their surroundings. The dam would have been exempted had construction already been underway.

In early 1971, the Corps announced that groundbreaking would be delayed while an environmental impact statement was drafted. In July of that year, U.S. Representative Pete du Pont of Delaware became the first major politician to break ranks with pro-dam forces when he unsuccessfully tried to remove money allocated for the first phase of construction because of environmental concerns. By May 1972, New Jersey Governor Tom Cahill concluded that the dam had become political poison and, parting ways with his fellow governors, outlined stringent environmental conditions that would have to be met before New Jersey continued to support the project.

Fisher became the leader of the Tocks Island squatters more or less by default because most were half his age. They fondly recall the little man walking through the valley from house to tepee to shack in all seasons. A natural born-teacher, he would stop to chat, in fact to dispense wisdom, often Lenni Lenape lore.

It is deeply ironic that the Corps gave squatters from New York City carte blanche to move into the homes and farms of River Rats and then hired other locals to raze these homes and farms. Inevitably, tensions between these two groups escalated into violence.

Carloads of vigilantes sped through the valley shooting out windows, setting fire to houses, barns and outbuildings, and killing pets and farm animals. In September of that year, Fisher demanded that Monroe County provide police protection. Before he could get an answer, armed federal marshals approached six squatter houses and a pup tent in bulldozers. The raid ended in a standoff when squatters climbed onto roofs and refused to leave. The result was a barrage of international news coverage that portrayed the corps and Poconos in an ugly light.

In July 1973, a federal judge ruled that the squatters were illegally occupying valley homes. In November, he gave them 30 days to vacate, but they refused. Finally, in the predawn hours of February 24, 1974 the standoff ended as 90 federal marshals pounced on 65 squatters, including a woman who had given birth the night before. The number would have been higher, but Fisher had been tipped off about the impending raid. Bulldozers quickly demolished the buildings, including several historic structures. One house was destroyed by accident.

The standoff was over, and for all intents and purposes so was the fight to build the dam as Eddie took deed to the Fox.

Shukaitis' group, the Sierra Club and other organizations obtained a restraining order stopping further destruction, while the federal budget that year contained no Tocks money for the first time since 1964. In 1975, the Delaware River Basin Commission, with the Corps' reluctant acquiescence, voted 3-1 to abandon Tocks. Only Pennsylvania Governor Milton Shapp, clinging to the canard that the dam would control flooding, still wanted to move ahead on a project that had triggered a civil war.

Although the otherwise modest Fisher wore his role in the Tocks victory like a big shiny badge, it also could be an albatross. When he and Eddie were confronted by a ranger while foraging for firewood in a state game land in the early hours of a blizzard, the ranger recognized the little man standing in snow that was nearly up to his waist.

"You're that fucking Tocks squatter fella," the ranger snarled.

Fisher stroked his chin and nodded.

"I don't know who your friend is," the ranger continued, "but I ought to throw the fucking book at you."

He relented only because the snow had begun falling even harder.

Chapter Five:

AMERICA STARTS HERE

Police Chief William Snow was a third generation Gap resident and the village's only full-time cop. Although he and Eddie had their disagreements and the bar owner was in on the Barney Fife jokes that were cracked behind Snow's back, the chief had been kind of fond of the man now lying in a pool of blood on the cellar ramp behind the Fox.

To be sure, Eddie could be a pain in the ass. Snow had to tell him to stop lobbing tennis balls from the Fox's second-floor porch onto the windshields of speeding trucks on Main Street, the only through road in a village with only a few side streets and a much-abused detour around Interstate 80 and the toll bridge over the Delaware River. Eddie responded by dragging a chair out into the middle of the street when school let out and engaged speeders with shouts and fist shakes.

Then there was the time Eddie and some friends were having an snowball fight outside the Fox and the bar owner winged a snowball at a village snowplow that Snow happened to be driving. Eddie was fined $51.

Snow had suspected that Eddie was behind the repeated destruction of a huge billboard advertising Saw Creek Estates, one of the first gated developments in the Poconos, that overlooked the toll booths from atop a dramatic tree-lined rock outcropping near where the Kittatinny House had stood. Gated developments betrayed Eddie's sense of community, besides which the billboard was an eyesore, but the village council did not share his sensibilities and refused a request to have it removed. Not long afterwards, the billboard was chain sawed down. When it was rebuilt it was chain sawed again, then replaced with a sturdier structure that in turn was doused with gasoline and set afire, and finally with a steel structure that outlived its nemesis.

Its heyday as a resort town many years in the past, the Gap had been atrophying for years and should have welcomed new blood. But many of the locals, notably Mayor Phil Farber and his determinedly mesozoic village council, did not take kindly to outsiders and the changes they might bring. Farber and the council would have been perfectly happy if there were walls at the ends of Main Street.

Virtually the only signs of life in the Gap were hikers like Owen Owen who crossed Main Street above the Fox on the Appalachian Trail. Some stopped for a bite to eat and a hot shower and a few like the Irishman lingered longer. But most continued on, perhaps sensing that they too were not particularly welcome. The village treasury was nearly empty and the regional Presbytery was on the verge of closing the Church of the Mountain because there were so few worshippers. There were the weekend crowds at the Deer Head Inn, but otherwise the Gap was stuck in time.

Even the Waring complex at the top of Main Street was a shadow of its once vibrant self. Although he was neither born nor raised in the Gap, Fred Waring had been a favorite son. The popular radio and television personality and leader of The Pennsylvanians was known as "The Man Who Taught America How to Sing." He also was a promoter, resort owner and financial backer who had brought to market that American kitchen icon, the Waring Blender.

Waring had taken over the Castle Inn, the last of the Gap's grand hotels, for his offices, publishing company and music and singing classes. But the inn was now derelict and its performance hall was little more than a brokedown palace that would serve as the backdrop for the stage at the first several years of the Delaware Water Gap Celebration of the Arts (COTA) before it was destroyed by fire.

In the eyes of Gap elders, who qualified as an insider versus who was an outsider was arbitrary.

Rick Chamberlain had been very much an outsider until he married the daughter of a former Gap mayor who owned the Deer Head Inn. Eddie, frustrated over the glacial pace of change in the Gap, goaded Chamberlain into running for council. He won by a single vote.

At the time of Eddie's murder the Gap could boast that it probably had more jazz clubs per capita than any community anywhere and an astonishing number of world-class jazz musicians as residents. But while that had considerable currency in the jazz community, most locals could care less, although some complained about the music.

That music could be heard at the Deer Head, as well as the Blue Note at the foot of Foxtown Hill in the Gap, and at the Fox.

This abundance of riches was a happy consequence of a resort industry that was booming (although its heyday would soon be over) and pretty much can be traced to one man, Bob Newman, who played tenor saxophone in Woody Herman's legendary Thundering Herd big band before leaving the road and becoming music director at the Mount Airy Lodge. Newman put together house bands during the 1960s and 70s that would back the biggest stars of the era, some of whom would play Mount Airy and other big resorts on a Saturday night and then appear on the top-rated *Ed Sullivan Show* in New York City the next night.

While some members of Newman's house bands were local musicians, others had established careers and were lured out Route 46, the main drag between New York and the Poconos before Interstate 80 opened, because of well-paying resort gigs and a vibrant late-night jam session scene.

"A musician leaving Mount Airy for New York had to drive by the Deer Head to get to the Portland Bridge and Route 46," says Patrick Dorian, the Distinguished Professor of Music at East Stroudsburg University, jazz historian and trumpet player.

"'Let's have a taste,' they'd say, and end up jamming until five in the morning with John Coates Jr. and other Deer Head regulars.

"'What a nice little club,' they'd say. 'What a nice little town. I could live here.'"

Coates, a pianist who has played at the Deer Head on and off since he was a teenager in the 1950s, was a major influence on jazz icon Keith Jarrett, who washed dishes at the Deer Head over several summers when he was in high school. Comedian Jackie Gleason, a frequent golfer at Shawnee, adored Coates and used to slip through the back door of the club to hear the gifted improviser, who remains active at age 72.

In 1962, Bob Dorough became one of the first musicians to move to the area. Dorough is a world famous practitioner of vocalese, a genre of jazz singing using melodies that originally were part of instrumental compositions, as well as the brains and voice behind the witty lyrics on "Schoolhouse Rock!," the *ABC-TV* children's show of the 1970s and 80s.

Then there was Morris Cohan, the father of actor Peter Coyote and a New York City broker who represented the interests of many musicians. Cohan bought a farm near the Gap and encouraged his musician clients to take advantage of the cheap housing prices and relatively close proximity to the Manhattan clubs that were their bred and butter.

Among the other musicians who joined Dorough were tenor saxophonist Al Cohn, trombonist Urbie Green, pianist-vocalist David Frishberg, bassists Steve Gilmore and Russ Savakus, woodwind artists George Young and Jay Cameron, keyboard player Wolfgang Knittel, and drummers Bud Nealy and Bill Goodwin. Goodwin, who along with Gilmore played with alto saxophone great Phil Woods for many years, initially lived in the attic of Dorough's house and eventually lured Woods to the Gap.

Woods started COTA with Eddie and Chamberlain, built a lovely home that he would return to from his world tours with the greatest jazz musicians of the last 40 years, and has become the *éminence grise* for the local jazz scene. If imitation is the sincerest form of flattery, Woods can point to a legion of disciples over the decades while Waring, who had a penchant for showmanship and gimmickry, had few. Like Waring, Woods was not a local boy, but he has remained an outsider to many insiders although his musical accomplishments far overshadow Waring's and he has helped burnish the Gap's latter-day image as a community friendly to the arts.

Where Waring was syrupy smooth, Woods can be blunt and sometimes combative.

There was, for example, Woods' battle royal with Al Broda, the former owner of the Water Gap Country Club. The club's maintenance shop and garages were behind Woods' house and in warm weather he would be jolted awake at 5 in the morning by the sounds of tractors and mowers being started up. When Broda blew off Woods' complaints that he often didn't get home until nearly that hour, he took the efficacious step of standing beneath the owner's bedroom window at inopportune times and serenading him with screeching sax notes.

The reticence about outsiders was especially true of refugees from the Tocks Island squatter debacle.

Some squatters had returned to New York City after being evicted by federal marshals from homes and farms in the Minisink by the Corps of Engineers. Others migrated to West Virginia and Oregon where they joined or started communes, while some moved down valley to the Gap. The first few new businesspeople arrived about the same time. The Sundance leather goods store opened, followed by Omega, a health-food store, then a pizzeria, consignment shop, tea room and art gallery as long empty Main Street storefronts came back to life and the Gap once again became a destination, not someplace to pass by or through.

Eddie had been introduced to the Poconos on his trucking routes from North Jersey. The "America Starts Here" sign just past the I-80 toll plaza at the Delaware River bridge was an appealing come-on for a man whose midlife crisis had arrived right on schedule and was desperate to get away from a failed marriage and a job with a union that to his disgust had been taken over by organized crime.

North Jersey Teamsters locals were now controlled by Russell Buffalino, a Mafia boss who ran the rackets in the Scranton area to the west of the Poconos and had considerable sway in North Jersey and New York, as well. Buffalino was no friend of truckers and had helped mastermind a scheme in which leasing companies were allowed to hire drivers at below-scale wages. The union was, in effect, a big piggy bank for the mob boss, who would be linked to the disappearance and presumed death of national Teamsters President Jimmy Hoffa in 1977.

Eddie fell hard for the Poconos and the faded beauty of the Gap, rented a place in nearby Cherry Valley with a friend and began looking for a business to buy.

The Fox was a cigarette smoke-stained dump. The electrical and plumbing systems were in especially parlous condition, but with some help from his brother Phil he bought the place at a sheriff's sale in 1974 for an affordable $26,800. The location seemed right and the business came with a coveted hotel license, providing a second source of income from renting out the rooms on the second floor.

The Fox wasn't much to look at: A three-story clapboard-over-brick corner building with a porch on the second floor, faded red paint and drooping gutters on the windward side, and a small parking lot off Oak Street behind it. There was a 12-stool bar, a kitchen and rest rooms on the first floor, five rooms and two baths on the second, and an apartment with a living room, kitchen, two bedrooms and a bath on the third where he would live. The floor sagged near the bar, but that's where a pool table would go.

Eddie's father-in-law had owned a bowling alley and bar

and he thought that the Fox was just about perfect for a business that would be a bar and restaurant by day and a bar and music club at night. There also was an unexpected bonus for a man who claimed to have Native American blood – the legend that the building was haunted by spirits because it had been built on a Minsi burial ground. He thought that was very cool.

The Cherry Valley Inn, the original business at the location, had been opened to take advantage of the fact that the Quaker-run Gap resorts did not have liquor licenses. Farber had owned the bar after World War II. He sold it to Tommy Cullen, a clarinet player who toured with Waring and The Pennsylvanians. Cullen already owned a restaurant called the Top of the Fox at the top of Foxtown Hill on the road linking the Gap to Stroudsburg and had renamed the place the Bottom of the Fox.

With the help of family and friends, including Bill Reinhart, Lloyd Miller and Al Ambler, all able carpenters, Eddie set to work gutting the bar. The floor was reinforced, the bar transformed from a straight 12-stool shot to a three-sided affair with about 20 stools, and a modest bandstand was built in a corner.

Eddie encouraged Reinhart to set up a wood shop in the Fox's cellar. Although the roar of the veteran's big Craftsman table saw sometimes drowned out the conversation upstairs, the booths and chairs that came out of the shop were one of Eddie's more successful efforts to spiff up the Fox, as well as a good project for the over-amped veteran to channel his considerable energies into.

The spartan walls and ceiling were gradually filled with beer mugs, mirrors, signs, deer antlers, a lava lamp and all sorts of other stuff.

The resulting cross between hippie chic and country and western was fitting because the two most popular bands that Eddie booked were Asparagus Sunshine, which leaned toward psychedelic and improvisational music, and Potbelly Stove, a rockabilly ensemble. Both invariably packed the Fox to the rafters.

Then there was the jukebox, an eclectic mix of the popular songs of the moment, some jazz and obscure titles, including a Fox favorite -- "The I-95 Asshole Song" by August and the Spur of the Moment Band -- a hilarious ballad about a trucker who gets run off the road by a wacked-out driver

Eddie ran through employees at a fairly steady clip early on. He fired the people who were more interested in drinking than working or helping themselves to the till, and the Fox eventually had a cadre of employees who would stay with him for years. One was a fiery woman who thought nothing of coming around the bar, taking someone by their shirt collar and marching him outside with instructions to not come back in until he could behave himself.

Miller recalls pulling into the Fox's parking lot one evening with Eddie. The bartender had pinned a regular to the ground, a clenched fist in the air, and was giving the offender a piece of her mind.

Miller paused after getting out of the car, but Eddie put a hand on his shoulder. "She can take care of herself," he laughed as he ushered Miller inside.

Snow never bought into the notion advanced by Farber and others that the new Fox was a magnet for trouble and the hippie owner was the cause. After all, there had been loud music and rowdy behavior when Cullen owned the place, and some of Cullen's regulars returned to the Fox when Eddie reopened it. But the music was Dixieland and not folk or rock, while Cullen was a local boy, not a long-haired outsider who had breached those invisible walls at the ends of Main Street.

The chief, like Eddie, had once been a truck driver, and like Eddie he respected the spirit of the law more than the letter. Snow knew that there sometimes was drug dealing in the parking lot behind the Fox. He had accompanied state Liquor Control Board agents on raids to snare underage drinkers and had corralled more than a few drunks who relieved themselves behind bushes on Main Street or were regurgitating last call.

Still, the drunks often lived in the Gap. Snow knew that Eddie would try to sober them up with a mug of coffee or soup before showing them the door, and he was more inclined to give them a ride home than lock them up. Just like Barney Fife.

Chapter Six:

THOSE BALEFUL BROWN EYES

Eddie quickly became the object of many a woman's affections. He could look like an unmade bed, didn't have the best teeth, usually wore a bandanna or hat because he was self conscious about a bald spot toward the back of his head, and had a lifestyle that was not always conducive to good hygiene. But he invariably was the center of attention whether he wanted to be or not.

Being bedded by the owner of the Fox had a certain currency among the popsies who competed for his attention and the men who competed for theirs, and he had a reputation for being great in the sack.

Some of his conquests were married, while one girlfriend in particular was the focus of envy -- and jealousy -- among the women whose orbit included the Fox because she liked to lean on the railing of the second-floor balcony when the bar opened in the morning in a state of dishabille, typically in a nightgown that barely covered her private bits, which many a male regular arriving for their first brew of the day noted were cosseted by neither bra nor panties. There obviously also was more going on behind Eddie's baleful brown eyes than he liked to let on, and their incandescence would sometimes let him down when he would try to strike a nonchalant pose.

One of Eddie's conquests wondered if she was really in love with him or merely with the idea of being in love with him. She guessed the latter, which was fortunate because any hopes that romps between the sheets would lead to something more serious were invariably squelched. He had never divorced after an acrimonious breakup with his wife, and had no interest in remarrying, let alone fathering more children. Nor did he open up to his lovers. True confessions were reserved for Rosalie Sorrels, neighbor Dotsie Hauser and one or two other women with whom he was not romantically involved. He sometimes was driven out of the Fox and up Main Street to Hauser's house by women who were chasing him, but in reality was rather lonely despite having so many friends and lovers.

Few people knew of Eddie's past except for his failed marriage, and this was only because his estranged wife had a habit of calling the Fox late at night as well as making an occasional unwelcome personal appearance, usually when she was on a bender.

Eddie's father was James W. Joubert, a highly decorated World War I infantryman of French descent who was assigned to the American 30th Division. The division, nicknamed Old Hickory because of its Southern roots, was the first to break through the Hindenburg Line. It fought its way across France and on October 10, 1918 defeated a German division in a ferocious battle at the village of Saint-Souplet near the Belgian border in one of the last major actions of the war.

James was awarded the Croix du Guerre (Cross of War) by France and Belgium for his bravery and came home to a hero's welcome in Duluth, Minnesota, where he met and married Agnes Gibson, an Irish immigrant. They later moved to Elizabeth, New Jersey where Eddie, Phil and a sister were born.

A family member says that James probably suffered from what today is recognized as post-traumatic stress disorder and was in poor health when he died of a brain aneurism when Eddie was 12, leaving Agnes Joubert to raise their three children. Both of James' sons were tightly wound, and the family member believes that their father's condition -- a consequence of the traumas that James' experienced on the battlefield and a hardscrabble life in Elizabeth -- accreted to them.

Eddie dropped out of high school, served a brief stint in the Air Force, and met and married his wife in Elizabeth. They moved to an old stone house on a small farm in rural Somerset County, New Jersey after the birth of their children.

There was a big garden and horses, goats and chickens. Both parents were fond of singing and dancing. Folk music, especially Peter Paul and Mary, Simon and Garfunkel, Joan Baez and Laura Nyro, was a favorite. But alcohol became a drag on the marriage and it ended with a crash when Eddie came home one day and found his wife in bed with a friend.

Eddie quickly became involved in the Poconos Tavern Owners Association and village affairs.

The owners included Anne Davies, who ran the Blue Note, at the foot of Foxtown Hill, Hans Hunsicker, who operated the Blue Bugle, a gay bar in Stroudsburg that had a largely straight clientele during the day, John Flood of Flood's in Stroudsburg, Steve Jacabowitz of the Tannersville Inn, Teddy Platt at Weery's, and Jay Thurman, who ran the Palace, a black bar in Stroudsburg with whom Eddie occasionally would go into New York City to play poker.

A friend joked that Eddie had better parenting skills than half the parents in the Gap and his affection for and interest in village youngsters was immediately apparent.

He helped organize a youth group for teenagers who had little to do. He gave rides to kids whose parents were working or couldn't afford cars, would clear off Lake Lenape up on the Kittatinny next to the Appalachian Trail when ice-skating season began and pestered the volunteer fire company to hose down the surface to make it glassy smooth. Bill Cohea, the minister at the Presbyterian Church of the Mountain, wanted a gazebo, so he rounded up the materials and organized carpenters to build one. There were large cracks in the sidewalk in front of Hauser's place that filled with water and iced up in the winter. He humped a wheelbarrow of leftover concrete from a project at the Fox up Main Street and the cracks vanished.

The jazz festival and Chamberlain's entry into Gap politics were other products of Eddie's energy. He rallied support to address the village's broken down sewer system, a perennial problem that warranted more mentions in one book on the history of the Gap than its golden age of tourism. The sewers were less a system than a web of wildcat lines, and in an effort to finally confront the issue, Eddie, Chamberlain and others combed the neighborhood pouring variously colored dyes into toilets to see where the flushed waters came out.

"You'd put dye in someplace and it would come out underneath a sidewalk, at what became the jazz festival site, or in the river," Chamberlain recalled. "Different colors, different places. It was pretty comical."

The upshot was the eventual construction of a multi-million dollar treatment plant funded by the state and county.

Eddie also helped start Monroe County's first curbside recycling program after he and Chamberlain found a way to retrofit the Gap's garbage trucks with bins. Endlessly inventive, he hit on the idea of cutting a hole in the floor behind the Fox's bar so bottles could be dropped into a 55-gallon drum, which would then be rolled out of the cellar to the curb for recycling. For a few days, the regulars delighted in hearing the thunk of glass whenever a bartender dropped Miller and Pabst bottles through the hole.

The delight turned to hilarity when the drum filled up and Eddie tried to roll it outside. The drum was so heavy that not even two people could budge let alone carry it to the curb. So it had stayed in the cellar, a monument to good intentions.

Darryl "Skinny" Pierson and Ray Meehan had wandered out into the parking lot on that mild late November evening to have a smoke a while after Eddie had gone out to fetch something from the cellar, but nothing seemed amiss and they waved to Snow as he drove by in his white Ford Fairlane police cruiser.

A few people trickled in from Linda Fogel's wedding reception. Richie Roche, a folk guitarist who was to be the evening's entertainment, arrived and began setting up.

The fact that Roche even was at the Fox was something of a personal triumph. It also was a product of Eddie's caring nature, which had been nurtured growing up in a working class neighborhood where one neighbor's problem was viewed by all as the neighborhood's problem.

Roche had made a brief run at college and then went off to Alaska where he cultivated a fondness for hard liquor. Eddie had opened the Fox a few weeks before his return. He fell into the scene and soon was a regular.

Roche's drinking soon raged out of control. He was binging on a quart and a half of Irish whiskey and Scotch a day and was well into the proverbial butt of Malmsey when Eddie intervened.

"Look, alcoholics pay a lot of my bills, but I love you," he had told Roche. "I'll never tell you that you can't come in here, but I can't serve you anymore."

Roche took the cure and Eddie eventually asked him to rejoin the Fox family, something that Roche is very proud of to this day.

The weirdness that Saturday evening was apparent the moment Roche walked through the front door. For one thing, Eddie was supposed to work but hadn't been seen for several hours. For another, there was a young couple with a child sitting at the bar heatedly arguing.

When Eddie still hadn't appeared, someone suggested that Chief Snow be called, but that didn't get anywhere. After all, Eddie knew how to take care of himself.

Chapter Seven:

HE'S DEAD, WE CHECKED

The first rule of a murder investigation is to protect the crime scene, but the area around Eddie already was a well trod mess by the time Chief Snow wheeled his police cruiser into the parking lot of the Fox. Blood was everywhere, including the shoes of the people who had run from the bar after the body was found.

It remains somewhat unclear exactly who made the gruesome discovery, which is not surprising considering the horror of the moment. There also are conflicting accounts about when Eddie disappeared and who and how many people were at the Fox, as well as recollections from a few people who asserted they were there but were not.

Some people say that bartender Joanne Jones found the body after she became increasingly concerned that no one had seen her boss for hours and went outside to look for him. But most say it was Darryl Pierson, who had asked the young couple who were arguing to leave.

According to this version, Pierson followed the couple outside to make sure they did leave, saw a body at the bottom of the cellar ramp and stumbled back into the bar ashen faced and nearly speechless, blurting "Out back! . . . Out back!" Regulars Joe Keiper and Darryl Knecht then ran outside and confirmed that it was Eddie.

Snow parted the people standing over the ramp and approached the body. His back bothered him whenever it was cold, and it was starting to get cold.

"They sure made a mess of him, Chief," someone volunteered.

"He's dead, we checked," someone else said.

"There's an ax sticking out of a bush behind Mildred's house," a third person offered, referring to the house next to the Fox. Snow nodded, couched down and played the beam of his flashlight over the body. Yes, Eddie certainly appeared to be dead.

Starting at what remained of Eddie's head, Snow noted a large V-shaped gash that began between the bridge of the nose and left eye and opened out into a wide chasm over the forehead. There was a sizable pool of purple-red blood below and behind the head about three feet in length and blood splatters on the basement wall. The force of the blow had shattered Eddie's upper denture, and a tooth had been knocked onto his jacket. His eyes were open, but had rolled back into his head. At first glance, it appeared that he had raised his left arm in a futile attempt to fend off his killer, but Snow knew better. Eddie might have been a scrapper, but he hadn't had a chance to defend himself in his last fight.

Snow held the beam on the left wrist. Hair from Eddie's scalp was imbedded in the wound, indicating that a second blow had been delivered after the initial blow to the forehead, which Snow suspected had killed him outright. Despite the gaping wrist wound, there was almost no blood there because he had bled out quickly from the adrenalin rush of the attack, which had sent his heart racing so hard that it pumped virtually all of his blood through the massive head wound in only a few seconds. And while there was another sizable wound on his left thigh visible through a tear in his jeans, again there was almost no blood. Yes, the chief was quite certain that he had been unable to fight back.

Eddie had been dead for a while. He was cold to the touch and his facial muscles were becoming rigid in the grotesque slow-motion dance known as rigor mortis. Snow also noted purple discoloration at the ends of his fingers that were signs of lividity, a condition caused by dilation of the blood vessels that is impossible to see until two hours or so after the heart stops beating. There didn't seem to be a weapon anywhere near the body, at least not that the chief could see with his flashlight, although it was obvious that the instrument that had dispatched Eddie was heavy and sharp. Like an ax.

Snow again played the beam across the body.

The chief had a hunch that the killer knew his victim or at least his victim's habits, and was aware that if the first axe blow did not take Eddie out, he would fight back with everything he had. Snow later surmised that the killer also had known that Eddie would be working virtually alone on an afternoon and evening when many Fox employees and regulars would be at Linda Fogel's wedding and reception, meaning that there would be far fewer people hanging around than on a typical Saturday. This premeditation became all the more obvious when someone noticed that the light over the back door that Eddie had thought was burned out as he headed for the cellar for the last time actually had been unscrewed.

What's more, robbery did not appear to be a motive. The killer couldn't have missed the big wad of money that had been knocked most of the way out of the breast pocket of his flannel shirt. In fact, including the cash in two other pockets, he was carrying $1,100 in bills, as well as some loose change. This was typical of Eddie, who preferred to carry the Fox's till on him rather than leave it unattended. No, the killer had not merely wanted to disable or rob Eddie. It was like he had been murdered several times over.

"Chief, you'd better come here."

It was Keiper, one of the Vietnam veterans who hung out at the Fox. The other vets included wild men like Bill Giese, a former infantryman who looked like Jesus, had a fondness for Russian roulette and was haunted by the memory of a Vietnamese mama-san he had killed, or Bill Reinhart, who would get so wasted that he had been flagged from the Fox for life, a signal accomplishment considering the antics that Eddie tolerated in his friends. Keiper had been an Army medic and stayed cool no matter the circumstances. He helped out around the bar when Eddie was short handed, was a sometime tenant of one of the second-floor rooms, and had a knack for remembering faces and names.

Snow, still kneeling, turned to Keiper.

"What's up, Joe?"

"There was a man and a woman. They had a baby with them. They were mixing it up right before we found Eddie. They're fixing to leave. Maybe you want to talk to them."

"Who are they, Joe?"

"I don't know, Chief. They're not from around here. They

were at the bar and were going at it pretty good."

"Thanks," Snow replied softly. He stood up with a practiced weariness. Now his back really hurt.
The investigation would be out of Snow's hands as soon as detectives from the state police barracks at Swiftwater arrived, and that wouldn't be a moment too soon. Snow wasn't the territorial type, but it never was a good day when the Staties had to be called in.

The chief suspected that the man and woman with the child had nothing to do with the murder. He was much more interested in seeing the ax in Mildred's bush, but he caught up with the couple, asked a few questions and then waved them on. He was walking back to the cellar ramp as a Gap Volunteer Fire Company rescue truck topped with floodlights pulled into the yard behind the Fox. The area was suddenly bathed in a brilliant white light, catching Snow, Keiper and others in a ghostly stop-action pantomime.

Word of Eddie's murder spread quickly.

Nurses in the emergency room at Pocono Hospital heard the call for the county coroner to be dispatched to the scene of a homicide in the Gap and made preparations should there be other casualties.

People lined up at the pay phone in the Fox to call Eddie's relatives and friends, while Ann Davies got the news when a breathless Ronnie Heller, who was driving past the Fox in his tow truck when he saw all the activity, ran into the Blue Note and broke the news.

"You'll never believe what happened," Heller said to Davies in hushed but excited tones. "Someone killed Eddie Joubert!"

Several present and former Fox employees had driven to the Blue Note after the wedding reception. Davies herded them into the kitchen where she broke the news.

Robbie Asmus, who was eight months pregnant, had gone home after the reception and was drifting off to sleep when cars pulled into her driveway. It was several friends who wanted to tell her in person.

The big question, of course, was who could have done such a thing.

"People started pointing fingers," recalled one Fox regular, "but it became pretty obvious pretty damned quickly that nobody we knew was involved because they were with us all afternoon and evening."

Chapter Eight:

THE GETAWAY

The second rule of a murder investigation is to take names, but the state police didn't seem particularly interested in doing that.

There was no chance that the killer had done the deed between the wedding and reception or afterward, and no chance that he had stuck around. It also was unlikely that he had slipped away, cleaned up and returned to the scene of the crime like a pyromaniac who sets a fire and then gets his rocks off watching firefighters race to the scene. No, it didn't figure that whoever had filleted Eddie was among the people that Tom Mastruzzo and Al Drozdowski, the first state police detectives on the scene, should have talked to. Still, there always was a chance that somebody had seen or heard something. But rather than take the names and telephone numbers of people in the crowd around the ramp, which swelled as people rushed to the Fox from post-wedding reception parties, they only took a few and then told everyone to beat it.

Mastruzzo and Drozdowski were soft spoken and seemed too low key to be cops, an attribute that held Mastruzzo in good stead when he dressed as a hippie and went undercover for drug stings. Both men were assigned to Swiftwater, the nearest state police barracks, which then and now has a high turnover rate attributable to morale problems and the Poconos not being seen as a choice assignment or a means of advancement for up-and-coming troopers. In a knuckheaded decision to save money that accelerated the turnover rate, headquarters in Harrisburg offered buyout packages to senior officers. Both men accepted.

Swiftwater was thus robbed of its most experienced if not necessarily best hands at a time when the Poconos was in the first throes of a crime wave that was a product of the region's metamorphosis into a bedroom community as new residents arrived with their feuds, addictions and other problems.

The ruggedly handsome Mastruzzo had been out with his wife celebrating their wedding anniversary, while the professorial-looking Drozdowski had been at home watching TV when the call came in that there had been a homicide in the Gap. Hard on their heels came Phil Joubert, then Robbie Rosenblum, Bob Allen, Dave Thomas and George Arnold.

Phil was seven years younger than Eddie and had the same vaguely aquiline looks. Otherwise they couldn't be more different. Eddie was tough on the outside and soft on the inside. Phil, whom a friend described as having a sort of "crushedness" about him, was soft all the way through and had a melancholy air about him no matter the situation or setting. He had been born on an April Fools Day, was a sucker for being teased and his feelings were easily hurt. Although he owned a piece of the Fox, no one thought of the popular hangout as Eddie's *and* Phil's place even though he would bartend and do maintenance. He never got over his brother's murder and his own divorce and killed himself in a clumsy but successful second attempt nine years later. One of his sons also was to commit suicide.

Rosenblum, a defense lawyer with a penchant for unsavory clients and unpopular causes, as well as occasionally the contraband that some of those clients trafficked in, had been called away from his third or fourth after-dinner Scotch. A Philadelphia native, Rosenblum had represented anti-Vietnam War protesters right out of law school. He toyed with the idea of a political career, but was put off by the pettiness of Philadelphia Democratic machine politics and moved to the Poconos.

Rosenblum's first law office was one of the booths built by Bill Reinhart. His second law office was in Stroudsburg, where he once fell behind on the rent and the landlord got a judgment to have him evicted. The landlord's lawyer was about to send the sheriff Rosenblum's way, but his secretary refused to type up the paperwork.

"She said Robbie was the finest lawyer she'd ever met and she wouldn't do it," a friend recalled.

After Philadelphia, practicing law in Monroe County was chump change for Rosenblum, and he made more than a few enemies, as well as many friends, because he was willing to take on judges, prosecutors and cops, seldom backed down and often won against formidable odds.

Rosenblum would let his sometimes destitute clients barter for his services. When Tocks Island squatter leader Glenn Fisher was arrested for drunk driving, which was compounded by him wetting his pants in the back seat of a police cruiser after the arresting officer refused his pleas to let him out, he paid Rosenblum with a bucket of fresh-picked wild blackberries. In fact, the lawyer's office was packed with furniture, sculptures, a truly awful painting of Grateful Dead leader Jerry Garcia, and other *objet d'art* from clients. Rosenblum also had helped out the Joubert family, and he and Eddie became close friends.

Bob Allen was Monroe County coroner and Dave Thomas his deputy. They have continued to alternate those positions to this day.

Allen is known for being an impeccable dresser. Whether it is 10 in the morning at the county courthouse or 10 at night on the cellar ramp of a bar in the Gap, Allen always was dressed to the nines. So it was an incongruous sight, this man who looked like he had walked off the pages of *GQ* stooped over the body of someone for whom freshly washed blue jeans and a Mexican wedding shirt was a fashion statement.

Rosenblum was a pretty spiffy dresser himself, although he never wore socks, even in the dead of winter. He had once embarrassed Allen during an especially acrimonious cross-examination at trial about the coroner's seeming obsession with what people wore.

"So you knew it was Mister So and So because he was wearing such and such?" Rosenblum asked.

"Yes," replied Allen.

"You're absolutely sure of that, Mister Allen?"

"Yes."

"And I suppose, Mister Allen, that you can tell the jury what color underwear you were wearing that day?"

The coroner never forgave the lawyer and made it a point

to tell people it seemed awfully strange that Rosenblum had gotten to the Fox on the night of Eddie's murder before he had. The implication was that Rosenblum knew Eddie had something illegal to hide and wanted to get rid of it before the law arrived.

It was probable that even if Eddie's killer was someone Joe Keiper might recognize, he had slipped away without being seen. That wouldn't have been hard to do. He could have melted into the trees and overgrowth behind the Fox obscuring a steep hillside that plunged about 30 feet to a swampy area and then Cherry Creek.

It hasn't been possible for many years to avoid using Main Street when leaving the Fox by car unless you use Cherry Valley Road, which begins across Main Street from the bar and meanders out through the lovely, eponymously named valley to points north and south.

But in 1981, someone who knew their way around would have had a good chance of getting out of town unnoticed without using Main Street or Cherry Valley Road. The trick was to use a Delaware River Bridge Authority service road only a few hundred feet behind the Fox that bypassed the bridge toll plaza and led to eastbound Interstate 80 and the bridge itself. Once on the New Jersey side of the river, the killer could take the cutoff to Copper Mine Road or continue on into New Jersey.

No matter the route, the killer probably was far away when Eddie's body was found. Or didn't go far at all because he was able to quickly reach his nearby home or that of a confederate where he could clean up, destroy his bloody clothes and stay out of sight.

Chapter Nine:

DARKNESS, DARKNESS

The third rule of a murder investigation is to protect the body. Bob Allen knew there was trouble on that count as soon as he saw Eddie.

For starters, Eddie was laying on a dirt and rock ramp contaminated with leaves, hemlock needles and trash from the bar, while the area around the body already was well trampled. The coroner stooped over Eddie, gave him a cursory look, stood up and straightened out his goose down vest.

"Let's get some photos, George."

George was George Arnold, a Coroners Office photographer who had shot every fatal car crash, arson fire and whodunit in the Poconos since the early 1960s.

A good crime-scene photographer tries to catch everything and miss nothing. This includes the scene, the area around the scene and possible entry and escape routes. Then there are photos of the victim, including full-body views, close-ups of wounds and physical evidence such as bloodstains, hairs and fibers, as well as additional photographs of the scene after the body is removed. Finally, there are surreptitious shots of bystanders since they might be witnesses or even suspects. Arnold was a pro, but there were no bystanders to photograph because Tom Mastruzzo and Al Drozdowski had sent them away. Arnold did snap off a couple of rolls of Eddie and the area around the cellar ramp – one in black and white and one in color -- before being escorted to the ax in Mildred's back yard.

The woman had settled out of court with one of Eddie's boarders when he sued her after his weimaraner allegedly died from eating dog food laced with rat poison in her back yard. Mildred would not have been considered a suspect, but it was deeply ironic that Eddie's attacker may have chosen the back yard of his most persistent nemesis to ditch the murder weapon.

Only a narrow alley separated Mildred's house from the west wall of the Fox, and she complained with quotidian regularity to the Gap council and anyone else who would listen about the noise from the day her new neighbor booked his first band.

It did not matter that the music frequently was acoustic folk and not at all loud. Eddie had covered the interior of the side wall with egg crate-like sound dampening panels, but Mildred continued to complain about the patrons if not the music. When her lawyer determined that the Fox was in violation of an ordinance requiring businesses with live music to be no closer than six feet from the curb line, Eddie moved the front wall of the Fox back a couple of feet, boarded up the front door and built a new entrance on the Oak Street side with a door made of barn wood and strained glass with a deer antler handle. He had a friend paint a poem on the inside. It read:

> A SLAM OF THE DOOR
> AND A LOUD GOOD NIGHT
> WAKES UP THE NEIGHBORS
> AND THAT AIN'T RIGHT

The complaints didn't stop and the village government began harassing Eddie.

"No Parking On This Side Of Street" signs suddenly appeared one day on the Fox's side of Main Street, reducing the number of parking spaces available to patrons. When Eddie and Dotsie Hauser, a friendly townie and daughter of a former Gap postmaster and diner owner, showed up at a village council meeting to inquire about the signs, Mayor Farber informed them that the cars were obstructing the view of motorists on Cherry Valley Road.

Hauser interrupted the mayor to note that vans with canoes on their roofs owned by the Pack Shack, a Delaware River expedition company, were allowed to park on Main

Street and they surely were obstructing traffic if anything was.

Several people, knowing that Farber had been caught out, tittered. Just then there was an enormous clap of thunder, the lights went out and Eddie's supporters stood up and applauded. The signs came down two days later.

The detectives found that while there was an ax handle with tired-looking duct tape on the business end sticking out from the bush, the head had been broken off. A cursory search failed to turn up said head, although Joe Keiper pointed out some footprints leading from Mildred's back yard to the hill that descended to Cherry Creek. The detectives didn't seem interested. The area beyond the yard was not searched, let alone gone over with a metal detector, to try to flush out an ax head or anything else of interest.

The investigation had hardly begun but it already was falling apart.

Things were getting downright silly up on the third floor of the Fox where Robbie Rosenblum was standing behind Drozdowski as the detective tried to get into Eddie's apartment. The door was locked. It figured. The lawyer knew that Eddie was uptight about his privacy in a building that was mostly bar and part boarding house. He had climbed the narrow steps to his apartment more than a few times to find a friend or drunken patron wandering around inside or screwing someone on his couch or bed. Rosenblum's postprandial buzz had disappeared and he sensed that the detective was keenly interested in finding out whether there were drugs stashed in the apartment.

Rosenblum knew that no one had a key except for the man about to depart for the Pocono Hospital morgue in the back of Allen's station wagon, and he nervously joked about how cops dealt with locked doors in the movies.

"How?" the detective asked.

"With their shoulder."

"That's a problem, Robbie."

"Why?"

Pointing to the hinges, Drozdowski replied tartly, "Because the door opens out."

A crowbar was found and after a few tries the door opened with a splintery pop. The apartment was dark and smelled of cigarettes.

Rosenblum knew that Eddie didn't deal drugs. And guessed that the detectives already had defaulted to the view the Fox's owner was dead because he did. Some of Rosenblum's clients certainly did deal drugs, and he figured that he knew more about trafficking in the Poconos than practically anyone regardless of whether they wore a badge or not. He would have known if there was heavy shit going on at the Fox, but there wasn't. Surely his good friend would have come to him if he was in trouble.

Rosenblum didn't think Drozdowski would find anything incriminating, but now he wasn't so sure and realized he was sweating despite the chill on the third floor as the detective turned on the lights and began working his way through the living room.

"Hmm."

"Find something?" Rosemblum asked.

Drozdowski nodded and pointed into a flower vase. Inside was a single thin marijuana cigarette.

The apartment was otherwise contraband free, but the joint was all the detectives needed to confirm their view that drugs had led to the murder.

It was true that Eddie seldom refused a puff or a line of cocaine or methamphetamine, and beyond having all the sex he could handle, another of the perks of being this particular bar owner was being gifted a joint or a small bag of white powder. It was an honor of a sort to go upstairs or out on the porch to get high with him. It also was true that a man who was usually steady did occasionally overindulge.

For this reason Eddie would charter a bus on St. Patrick's Day for he and his friends to go bar hopping. Although there had been no bus tour the St. Patrick's Day before his murder, he more than outdid himself. High on meth, he began flipping out after speeding for a couple of days. He threw money around the bar and hassled a customer when the customer tried to order some food. Later that evening, convinced that Indians were paddling up the Delaware to come after him, he burst into the second-floor room of an employee and became enraged when he found her boyfriend in bed with her.

Eddie charged back downstairs. Bartender Kate Holmes, Bill Reinhart and the several other people present ignored him until he pulled a baseball bat out from behind the bar and began batting billiard balls at them. Then he pulled out a rifle. Holmes cleared the bar and called Teddy Platt, the biggest person she knew, a mountain of a man who was a sometime cook at the Fox, but he didn't want to deal with

Eddie. She then summoned his brother Phil, who was able to talk him down and drive him to a friend's house where he was given a Valium and slept off his high. The Fox reopened two days later, but some people thought that Eddie had fried his brain and was never quite the same again.

Eddie's good-time zeal had been contagious when he first bought the Fox. He and his new friends would transform it into a place where there was good food, good music and good vibes. He gave away ballpoint pens as presents one Christmas with the name of the bar and a favorite saying that captured his once easy-going attitude: "If you can't make it, don't come."

The Fox finally was turning a modest profit, most of which was being put back into the bar with projects like a new floor under the pool table, an expanded food selection and a menu that was no longer scrawled on a chalk board but was listed on smart-looking printed menus. Some of the regulars joked that the Fox was becoming too respectable for them, although they needn't have worried.

Eddie always had been attentive to the Fox's food and would make some dishes himself, including a memorable cream of broccoli soup. He would go on runs to Rhode Island, where a favorite uncle lived, to buy bushel baskets of black Narragansett clams at a time when fresh shellfish was a rarity in the Poconos. He would steam the clams to perfection for pasta dishes and make delicious New England-style chowders.

The food was now good enough that the Fox was catering parties at Instrument Specialties, the Gap's only employer of any size. The once vilified outsider was now feeding the insiders and recently had been elected treasurer of the Gap Chamber of Commerce.

In the beginning the drugs of choice were marijuana and feel-good trips like psilocybin mushrooms or the occasional bag of peyote buttons that a regular would bring back from trips to the Southwest. But the days were long gone when Eddie would tell patrons that they could help themselves to a beer and leave money on the bar while he went upriver to swim at Smithfield Beach on hot summer afternoons.

The Fox had slowly and perhaps inevitably changed. It no longer put out energy but was sucking it in, and some regulars started to stay away. Some people said that it was the darkness of the mountain. People with giant Ls on their foreheads – as in L for Loser, as one bartender put it – slouched around the bar drinking beer and shots of tequila until they ran out of money and went home to houses without electricity or heat.

The biggest reason for the mood change was the arrival of coke and meth in the Poconos in quantity. The primary coke source in the Gap was a waiter at the Water Gap Country Club, while bikers typically supplied the meth.

The "big dust period," is what Reinhart called it as the idealism that had suffused the Fox was overtaken by the darkness of these drugs – and the mountain.

It also was a time of high anxiety in the Gap because of a series of arson fires, the most recent being the attempt to torch the duplex two doors down from the Fox several days before Eddie's murder.

The fire could have had tragic consequences had Shawn Joubert, the 16-year-old son of Eddie's brother Phil, not had a premonition that something was wrong while partying with friends late that night over at Minisink Hills. He was living in one of the second-floor rooms at the Fox, but would occasionally stay at the house with a wraparound porch that his father shared with a girlfriend. Linda Fogel, who had been married the day of the murder, lived in the other half of the duplex with her three young sons.

Shawn Joubert said nothing seemed amiss when he arrived at his father's house about 3 in the morning, but as he stood in the kitchen eating a piece of apple pie and drinking a glass of 7-Up he heard a "whoosh" on the back porch, which erupted into flames. He woke his father, his father's girlfriend and the Fogel family. The fire, which a fire marshal determined had been started with an accelerant, damaged the porch but not the duplex itself.

The likely back story to the arson was the molestation of one of Fogel's sons by a notorious local pedophile. Fogel chose to not report the incident -- a more typical response to such a crime then than today -- and the man was not arrested, although he was to do serious jail time on two occasions in future years for other incidents. But he was subjected to a roughing up that angered one of his brothers, who publicly threatened to blow up the house.

There was a time when you could get away with a lot at the Fox. Eddie told Reinhart to stay away on numerous occasions after he became too rowdy, but was never one to hold a grudge and continued to play in the Friday night poker games at Reinhart's place.

But the veteran's pertinacity for hell raising eventually got him kicked out for good after he stumbled into Eddie's apartment one night with a buzz on and proceeded to tease him about his bouts of paranoia.

Eddie sometimes believed that the police had tapped his phone, usually sat with his back to a wall so he could see who might approach him, used a one-way intercom to listen in on what was going on two floors down in the bar, and sometimes wore an eye patch and beret and called himself Jacques. The regulars weren't fooled, of course, but he could case out strangers of whom he was suspicious without giving himself away.

Angered, Eddie threw a table lamp at Reinhart without unplugging it, blowing a fuse and plunging the Fox into darkness. As Reinhart drove away, the lamp flew out a window and crashed down onto Main Street behind him.

It seemed all too appropriate in the closing months of Eddie's life when someone slipped a quarter into the jukebox and played B.B. King's cover of "The Thrill Is Gone."

> *The thrill is gone*
> *It's gone away for good*
> *Oh, the thrill is gone baby*
> *Baby it's gone away for good*
> *Someday I know I'll be over it all baby*
> *Just like I know a man should*

Chapter Ten:

THE AX FELL OFF THE ROOF

There are plenty of reasons why Eddie's murder might remain unsolved nearly 30 years on, but only one explains why it was doomed from the start.

This was because the state police had no interest in solving it. The victim was, in the vernacular, from the wrong side of the tracks and justice in Monroe County was like an adjustable wrench. A crude social calculus determined how that wrench was calibrated. If you were a "somebody" and met with foul play, it was more likely that your departure from the mortal coil of the Poconos would be taken seriously by police and prosecutors. It was Eddie's misfortune to be a middle-aged hippie who ran a bust-out joint in a one stoplight town and consequently he was not worthy of breaking a sweat over.

The victims in several other unsolved Poconos murders in the years before and after Eddie's also were undesirables according to that calculus – gays, drug dealers, gay drug dealers, or other "lowlifes." There were no arrests in all but one of the murders and while an assailant did jail time in that one, the motive has remained safely hidden. Until now.

In one case, the 1977 slaying of David Allen Gross, whose body was found at a scenic overlook above the Delaware River about two miles south of the Fox, the investigation limped along only because of the tireless efforts of his mother, while the one detective who showed real interest in finding her son's killer was taken off the case, reassigned to it years later and then taken off it again.

In the cases of both Eddie and Gross, investigators said privately that they knew who had killed them but did not have enough evidence.

That may be so with Gross, but in Eddie's case this was a seemingly earnest way for investigators to make it appear that they had done their jobs as best as they could, but because of circumstances couldn't quite get to the finish line. Truly diligent detectives like the Gross case investigator don't give up so easily. Not every murder can be solved. That noted, successful murder investigations take on a life of their own and traction is created through sheer doggedness. But there was no sustained effort with Eddie.

In fact, his murder was well on its way to becoming a cold case by the time his daughter Cheryl reopened the Fox after getting rid of the kitchen woodstove and anything else that was a reminder of an ax. She also forbade anyone from entering the cellar alone.

There were several theories about why Eddie had been murdered. They ranged from the sublime (he was silenced because he had blabbed about secret Indian rituals; and after all, an ax is just a big tomahawk) to the ridiculous (he was killed by the mob because he refused to pay ASCAP royalties for the copyrighted songs the bands at the Fox played) to the possible (he was killed by the enraged spouse of one of the many married women he bedded).

But it was obvious to the relatively few people the state police interviewed that they were convinced drugs were behind the murder, although Eddie's family and friends told them over and over that he was a casual drug user and not a dealer, and in fact had been coming down hard on dealing.

Eddie had told his employees to throw out anyone suspected of dealing, and to call Chief Snow if they got hassled, and he talked about building a house for his children, a refuge from the smell of stale beer and piss that would be a more suitable environment for daughter Cheryl and son Jimmy, who kept threatening to drop out of school. He knew that a drug bust would be the end of the Fox and his dreams, and not even a savvy lawyer like Robbie Rosenblum would be able to help. But despite having no evidence beyond a single slim joint in a flower vase, the investigators were uncurious about anything that didn't dovetail with their assumption.

Robbie Asmus, who as the Fox's kitchen manager and a longtime bartender probably knew the comings and goings of her boss and his extended family better than anyone, was interviewed only once and then only briefly.

"All they wanted to know about was drugs," she said.

Richie Roche said investigators were disinterested in talking about anything other than drugs.

Bill Reinhart sat for one cursory interview.

"They were really chasing the drug thing," he said. "They really had that mentality."

It was obvious to Lloyd Miller, who had been in the Fox the night of the murder, that investigators were going through the motions. They showed no interest when Miller said that he had his suspicions about a certain man with a temper so violent that he might resort to taking an ax to Eddie.

When Kate Holmes was interviewed, the questions again were limited to drugs. Holmes later received an anonymous phone call from a man who said that he had just been released from the Monroe County Prison, and had spoken

with an inmate who claimed that he knew who had killed
Eddie. She reported the call to the state police but they
never followed up on it.

A woman who had been living in a second-floor room at
the Fox told investigators that her boyfriend began act-
ing strangely after the murder, perhaps had seen or heard
something and suddenly decided to move away. He was
never interviewed.

Darryl Pierson had been catching a smoke near the cellar ramp about the time that Eddie disappeared. Pierson
offered to be hypnotized in the hopes that he might recall
something about the cars in the parking lot, but the detective to whom he spoke only was interested in talking about
drugs.

When one of the detectives was asked by another cop
why he wasn't having a state police specialist administer
lie detector tests, the detective replied that they weren't
admissible in court. When the cop then said that they were
nevertheless an effective way of sweating information out
of reluctant witnesses, the detective merely shrugged.

Joe Keiper also was interviewed only once, and then for
only a few minutes. But in a shocking turn of events
several years later, he was chatting with a Gap resident
who revealed that as a child he had made a pictograph of a

man killing another man with an ax after Eddie's death. It seemed possible from the crude drawing that Keiper was given that the then young resident might have witnessed the murder and had long repressed the memory.

Keiper took the pictograph to the business where one of the now retired detectives worked and gave it to him, but the detective did not follow up on this potentially promising lead.

So primed are people to see what they want to see and to reject what runs counter to their expectations that psychologists have coined a term to describe how they mislead themselves. Confirmation Bias, as it is called, is an especially serious handicap for homicide investigators. In Eddie's case, the investigation was skewed from the start because detectives latched onto anything that agreed with their drug bias while ignoring information such as the crude drawing that might have led them to another motive and the killer.

As far as the state police were concerned, their bias was more than confirmed when the results of the toxicology tests on Eddie's body came back. They revealed that he had a trace of cocaine in his blood and marijuana metaboloids in his urine that suggested he was a moderately heavy pot smoker.

Reverend Cohea, who had rescued the Presbyterian Church of the Mountain when it was on the verge of closing, connected with the owner of the Fox the first time they met. The minister had been an organizer in poor Chicago neighborhoods and Eddie a Teamsters organizer. Cohea saw burning within Eddie a tremendous creative energy. Once their friendship was established, Eddie threw himself into Cohea's ministry.

Eddie was not a churchgoer, but helped Reinhart and Miller build a gazebo next to the church and a hiker's center with a shower for people coming off the Appalachian Trail. He also helped put on church-community productions including *Jesus Christ Superstar*, *The Wiz* and Christmas Eve and jazz festival services, and would send troubled friends and acquaintances up Main Street for counseling. He was protective of the minister, never inviting him up to his apartment with other friends because he didn't want him exposed to drugs.

Cohea suffered a heart attack two years before Eddie's murder, resigned his ministry and built a chapel and spiritual retreat over the mountain that he named Columcille for St. Colum (later Latinized as St. Columba), who had built the original abbey on the tiny Isle of Iona between Ireland and Scotland in the 6th century. In a gesture of

al of Eddie, he and Rick Chamberlain
lay with a bottle of Champagne to celebrate
ning of Columcille. Despite all that Cohea had done
for the community, no one else from the Gap did anything
similar.

The minister and the bar owner discussed their respective spirit worlds at length. Time seemed to stand still -- the past receding and the future just beyond reach -- in those numinous moments they shared over a beer at the Fox or in Cohea's book-lined study at Columcille.

Eddie was not just another truck driver from the tough streets of North Jersey who could talk with his fists. While he was not particularly book smart and had dropped out of high school, he had an opaline mind and insatiable curiosity about the purpose of life and its spiritual underpinnings. He didn't merely tolerate differences in people, he revered them.

He would draw on Native American lore during his discussions with Cohea, exploring the energy of the mountain and how it sometimes could be dark. As befits a Libra, being in balance with the people and other creatures around him was important, and drove his involvement in community projects. He was not a water sign, but had the sensitivity and intuition of one, and was fascinated by the idea that Pocono waterways – from the smallest rivulet to streams like Cherry Creek -- flowed into ever larger waterways and eventually into the Lenape, the Minsi name for the Delaware and the one he preferred to use.

Owen Owen, in his own discussions with Eddie, quoted the French philosopher Blaise Pascal, who had said "Rivers are highways that move on, and bear us whither we wish to go." The young Irish hiker was teased about his seemingly endless supply of pithy quotes, but this one struck Eddie as being profoundly true.

Holmes was hit hard by the lackadaisical nature of Eddie's murder investigation some three years later.

She had continued working at the Fox and stayed on as a night bartender when Cheryl Joubert sold it to a local man who reopened the place as a nightclub called Rumours.

At the end of her shift one evening in 1984, Holmes wasn't able to find a ride home and called a cab.

"That's the old Bottom of the Fox," the cabbie remarked as he pulled onto Main Street. "That's where that guy was killed."

Holmes acknowledged that it was.

"You know what they say," the driver said.

Holmes asked who said what.

"The police," he replied, laughing. "You know what they say. The ax fell off the roof."

Chapter Eleven:

THE AWFUL SOMETHING

It had been obvious to Cheryl Joubert and her father's closest friends that he was in fear for his life in the days before his murder.

Eddie had lost his Libran cool and felt anything but balanced. He was afraid to sleep and was giving away his possessions. These included a cherished pair of water buffalo sandals and some Native-American jewelry, and he gifted several boxes of clothing to the Night Owl, a consignment shop up Main Street. Eddie was always working on something and had nearly finished installing French doors in his apartment, but now the project languished. He was unable to focus on running the bar except "to try to get some of his family more in tune with what was going on with the business," as one employee put it, while he told Kate Holmes to sign his name on checks when there were deliveries.

Even after Eddie's daughter got down on her knees and begged him to tell her why he was so frightened, he refused to do so. In all likelihood this was because he didn't want her to become a target, as well. While he told Robbie Asmus that he had found out about a "group" of people who had done "something awful," Rosalie Sorrels and one other woman apparently were the only people with whom he was more specific. He told Sorrels that the group was a child pornography ring. He elaborated a bit more when he spoke to the other woman, explaining that he "had stuck his nose into" the affairs of some people involved with "whips and chains and child porn."

In fact, these were gay men who engaged in sadomasochistic sex. Some members also used and dealt drugs.

The group included two prominent men. One, Dr. John Oliver Nelson, was a pillar of the Poconos community, an ordained Presbyterian minister who had taught at the Yale Divinity School and founded Kirkridge Lodge, a 400-acre complex of buildings off the Kittatinny Ridge about three miles from the Gap.

It was Nelson's view that the Presbyterian clergy in the U.S. was ossifying. He would hold workshops and retreats at Kirkridge where clergymen and women were encouraged to become more involved with their congregations, including joining them in manual labor and other activities. The lodge also included an alcohol and drug rehabilitation center at one time.

Kirkridge was Nelson's legacy, and at his death he was more or less penniless because he had plowed most of his family fortune into the lodge and many good works. But behind Nelson's warm smile and firm handshake were dark secrets. "Jack," as his friends called him, was a closeted homosexual who lured boys and young men, some of them runaways and some possibly rehab residents, into having sex with him. The minister, according to a friend of many years, came to his home on several occasions late at night bleeding and bruised after being brutalized during sex.

Nelson's thirst for boys and young men seemed unquenchable, and even in the years before his death at age 81 "he was still running around 'helping' youths," according to one acquaintance, who adds bemusedly: "High holiness and wild horniness, why do they pair so neatly?"

The second prominent man lives in the Lehigh Valley, immediately to the south of the Poconos, and had a reputation in the gay community for being especially vicious and sadistic.

Three and possibly four murders may be linked to these two men and their confederates. Two of the victims were gay and a third may have had sexual encounters with men for money, while two were doing drug deals when they were killed.

The first gay man was Bruce Mann, a 26-year-old plasterer, musician and sometime falconer whose death was ruled a probable suicide.

Hans Hunsicker, who was the godfather of the Poconos gay community and proprietor of the Blue Bugle in Stroudsburg, some of Mann's other friends and the evidence suggest a different story: They believe that he was shot in Mountainhome, north of Stroudsburg, on the evening of April 18, 1974 by one of three men whom he had met in connection with a drug deal. The friends say his body was placed in the back seat of his Volkswagen Beetle, which was driven to Pocono Summit in Tobyhanna Township and dumped behind his apartment.

A Pennsylvania State Police report states that Mann had been despondent because he owed his boss money, was drinking prodigious quantities of beer and wine and walked out into a wooded area behind his apartment where he shot himself through the right eye with his own .25-caliber pistol, pulverizing his brain. The report states that he had gone missing five days before his body was found and further notes that he was "known to engage in homosexual activity." This was shorthand for the police belief that gays were deviants and Mann's sexual orientation might be a factor in his demise.

If Mann was a suicide, it was a strange one to say the least.

Gunshot suicide victims typically put the muzzles of weapons in their mouths and don't aim them into their eyes at an unusual angle that is more indicative of a victim lying on the ground and an assailant standing over and shooting him in the face at close range. It also seems unlikely that Mann had shot himself five days before his body was found. The Pocono Summit area teems with wildlife ranging from black bears to carrion crows and vultures, and his corpse would not have lain undisturbed. Indeed, there is no indication in the police or coroner's reports that his body had been picked at. Furthermore, being despondent over a debt does not wash because Mann owed his boss only $900, while the claim that he was drinking heavily was debunked by a toxicology test that showed his blood-alcohol level was a mere 0.07 percent. Finally, the fact that Mann's pistol was clenched in his right hand means nothing; it is the oldest trick in the faked suicide book.

A more likely explanation is that Mann was marked for murder by or in connection with Dr. Nelson.

Hunsicker painfully recalled that he was supposed to meet Mann at his apartment the following day to share with him a favorite recipe for carrot soup. But Mann had frantically phoned him at the Blue Bugle on the evening of April 17 saying that he was in danger and before hanging up had blurted out, "If I get killed Dr. Nelson will know who did it."

The police report, which would not be public if it had not been annexed to the coroner's report, which is a public record, includes this cryptic paragraph in which Nelson neatly contradicts himself:

> Trooper called Dr. Jon Oliver Nelson. He said he didn't remember Bruce Mann. He recalled that he lived in a commune-type place with [names of two men].

The police report is a summary of accumulated information and has many holes in it. It is not stated why the state police sought out Dr. Nelson, although it can be supposed that it was based on their being told about the phone call. They did not follow up on Nelson's statement although it was contradictory on its face. This is because they washed their hands of Mann once his death was ruled as not being a homicide.

After all, he was just another queer.

The second gay man was Harry Read, an overtly effeminate 40-year-old bar owner with dyed blond hair, a goatee and high, squeaky voice, a nasty temper and world-class cocaine habit who fancied biker's denims and wore a turquoise stud in his right ear lobe.

Read told friends on March 31, 1983, some 16 months after

Eddie's murder, that he had sold to the second prominent man the Lucky Lady, a bar he owned across the Delaware River in Blairstown, New Jersey, as well as the trailer he lived in behind the House of the Rising Sun, another bar that he owned in Gilbert in the West End area of the Poconos. The second prominent man had done previous deals with Read and had once co-owned the House of the Rising Sun with him.

When Read told friends that he had consummated the deal but would not be paid the agreed-upon $35,000 until the next day, they expressed concern because of the second prominent man's reputation for violence. Read then produced a pistol and assured them that he would be okay.

Read would not be okay.

When 40-year-old Read and his 22-year-old lover were found lying on Pensyl Creek Road in Hamilton Township early the following morning, he was butchered beyond recognition and had been nearly decapitated, while the lover had been stabbed repeatedly to within an inch of his life.

It is likely that Read first was beaten about the head. The medical examiner who conducted a post-mortem examination found six separate bruises. He then was stabbed and slashed over 20 times in the temple, face, neck and chest, and there were so many cuts to his neck that his left jugular vein was exposed and his upper spinal cord was nearly severed. Unlike Eddie, he was able to fight back and there were defensive wounds on his right forearm, thumb and index finger.

Read's lover was stabbed 15 times but survived.

With a big assist from the second prominent man, state police quickly wrapped up the case. Or so they thought. Monroe County District Attorney James F. Marsh declared that the second prominent man had fingered Keith Michael Scott, 18, of Gilbert, whom the DA said Read had recently fired as a cook at the House of the Rising Sun. He described the teen as deeply troubled with a history of violence and drug and alcohol abuse. It later was learned that Read had given Scott drugs in return for homosexual favors.

Marsh acknowledged that there appeared to be no motive for the crime, while his assurances that only Scott was involved do not stand up to scrutiny in part because of the murky role of the second prominent man. (Scott eventually pleaded no contest and was declared incompetent to stand trial. He served a six-year term at Farview State Hospital for the criminally insane.)

The prosecutor said that Read and his lover were driving Scott from Gilbert to Route 33 so he could hitchhike to the

Lehigh Valley, which is to the south, but they were headed north when Scott, who was seated in the back seat of the second prominent man's Lincoln Continental, slashed Read's throat while the car was stopped on Pensyl Creek Road, a notorious gay lover's lane at the time.

Scott told police that he took 20 pain pills and drank two quarts of beer and some vodka before getting into the car with Read and his lover. It begs credulity how he could have slashed Read as his victim fought back, then pursued Read's lover in such a drugged and inebriated condition when one or both of the victims were out of the car, and then driven to Allentown in the Lehigh Valley, where he was arrested at a bus station a day later. All of this suggests that he may have had an accomplice.

The second prominent man provided police with a photograph of Scott that he claimed Read had taken at the House of the Rising Sun but was selective about what he told police and Marsh, including not disclosing that he had bought but not paid for one of Read's businesses and his trailer just hours before his death.

Chapter Twelve:

HE FOUND HIMSELF ADRIFT

The third murder victim who can be linked to the sex ring was David Allen Gross, whose body was found at a scenic overlook two miles from the Fox. Gross knew Dr. Nelson and possibly other members of the ring, while Hans Hunsicker had cashed a check from Nelson made out to Gross, as he had on previous occasions, on the night of the young marijuana dealer's murder.

The fourth victim may have been Eddie.

As depraved as the sex ring's members were, knowledge of the ring's existence in and of itself may not have been sufficient reason for Eddie to be murdered, although as someone who worked with, and was extremely protective of, young people, he would have been deeply angered that there were men in his midst who were preying on them. But there could have been another reason: He may have found out the identity of one or more of Gross's killers, who in turn learned that Eddie knew who they were and would have to eliminate him.

Is it merely coincidental that three of the victims had

contact with Dr. Nelson or the second prominent man, and Eddie may have learned their identities? Is it merely coincidental that while one victim was killed by gunshot, the other three were murdered with everyday objects and in ways that were particularly vicious and sadistic?

There is another possible similarity, as well: There were accomplices in the Read, Mann and Gross murders and the victim's body was moved from the crime scene in two of the three, or possibly all three. That might have been the intention with Eddie, as well.

Did the man with the ax have an accomplice who was waiting in the Fox's cellar? Did they plan to remove Eddie's body, perhaps in the back of his Volvo wagon, a vehicle that everyone knew didn't have a key and could easily be hotwired to start? Was it their intention to sew confusion by leaving the car elsewhere as had been the case with Gross, or remove it from the scene of the crime in the case of Mann?

Tall, thin and with hair too long for his father's conservative tastes, Gross had his parents' good looks. He liked cars, art and weightlifting, but like many a young man then and now, found himself adrift after breaking up with a longtime girlfriend.

Gross was certain about what he did not want: Continue to do masonry and carpentry work for his father and uncles in their construction business. But he was less certain about what he did want to do after he had quit. And so a few weeks into the summer of 1977 he took a low-paying job at a gallery run by a friend's parents, where he could pursue his artistic interests while planning his return to a far more lucrative line of work: Supplying the insatiable demand for marijuana in the Poconos.

His 21st birthday was on August 2, 1977 and he threw a big party four days later on property that his father owned next to Ice Lake in Barrett Township. There were two bands and kegs of beer. He had not dealt marijuana for a year or so but told several friends that he had lined up 120 pounds through what he called "new connections" and soon would be meeting one of those connections. He also said that he had several buyers, one of whom owed him several thousand dollars from previous deals but had promised to make good with the forthcoming one.

Gross was scrupulously fair, which is why friends had always bought pot from him, and he would become extremely upset when people tried to rip him off. He confided to his mother that he couldn't understand why people dampened an otherwise great time by stealing pitchers of beer at his birthday party. This boyish naiveté may have literally been a fatal weakness.

Late in the afternoon of August 9, a friend stopped by Gross's house and his mother made them roast beef sandwiches. Early in the evening, she left to go to a ceramics class and her son for Tamiment, a resort near Bushkill, where he would help hang pictures from the art gallery for a show. The empty kegs from the party were still in the back of his Chevrolet Nova hatchback. He had covered them with a canvas tarpaulin.

Gross, however, did not go straight to Tamiment. He stopped at the Blue Bugle where Hunsicker noticed that this usually calm young man seemed unsettled. Hunsicker cashed a $110 check made out to Gross by Dr. Nelson, who would add $10 or $15 to the checks. Ever the businessman, Hunsicker would get a cut for cashing the checks while Nelson knew that Hunsicker would be discreet about the arrangement.

When Gross didn't return home later that night his parents thought that he may have had too much to drink and didn't want to drive home, but when he hadn't appeared later on August 10 his mother started worrying. It wasn't like her son to not call. Besides which, it was her birthday and David would never miss her birthday.

It was shortly after 1:30 a.m. on August 11 when Upper

Mount Bethel Township Patrolman Granville Nolf noticed Gross's Nova parked at the Arrow Island Scenic Overlook, one of several small parking areas off of Route 611 in the Delaware Water Gap National Recreation Area just south of the Gap.

Nolf pulled up to the Nova, his police cruiser's headlights illuminating the car, and got out. The front doors were locked so he walked around to the back and tried to open the hatch. It too was locked, but something caught his eye: What appeared to be blood on a jumbled up canvas tarp. He looked closer and saw part of a bloodied head sticking out.

An autopsy determined that Gross was dead only a few hours after he had left Bushkill about 11 p.m. on August 9, and while there may be gaps in what he did during that relatively brief period, this much is apparent:

He had taken back roads from Bushkill and skirted the Stroudsburgs in driving in a southwesterly direction to an out-of-the-way location in Pocono Township where he picked up the marijuana. He split it into several smaller packages, two of which he left at the end of the long driveway to a home off of Sullivan Trail near Tannersville. He then retraced his earlier route from the other direction and arrived at a cottage on the northwestern edge of Stroudsburg sometime after midnight where, according to one theory, he walked into a trap.

At least two men were at the cottage, one possibly a confederate of the man who owed Gross money and the other a man who was about Gross's age and well on his way to earning a reputation in the community for violent and sadistic behavior. Both that man and Gross had been in the Fox, although they were never seen together.

A musician who was playing at the Fox regularly in 1977 said of the man: "You see people from the stage and you just know when they're weird."

According to another theory, Gross was fatally assaulted at a private residence elsewhere by a man who was to go on to commit another drug-related murder.

Like Eddie, Gross showed no signs of having struggled. The assailant apparently came up behind him and garroted him with a rope, twisted the rope to strangle him and then for good measure repeatedly struck him in the head with what probably was a hammer.

In what would have had to be an extraordinary coincidence if it had no connection to the murder, the cottage burned to the ground later that night.

Whether Gross was slain at the cottage or the private residence, his assailants took the marijuana and Gross's wallet and tore apart the interior of the Nova.

This would seem to have been an effort to find out whether any other contraband was on board, but there may be a more sinister explanation: The men, having destroyed the murder scene, were intent on destroying the check that had been written out to Gross by Dr. Nelson because it could lead investigators back to the instigators if not the murderers.

It is unclear where the car was left in the hours between the murder and when it was driven to the scenic overlook, where passersby later reported they had seen it several hours before Patrolman Nolf.

Meanwhile, the father of the man who owed Gross money used his influence as a district justice to protect his son by impeding the murder investigation. He threatened the trooper originally assigned to the case with an harassment lawsuit if he continued to investigate his son and threatened Gross's father when he confronted the district justice and his son.

The investigation of Gross's murder has played out in fits and starts over a 32 year period, and while it initially appears to have been as desulatory as Eddie's, substantial progress has been made because of the persistence of his mother and the work of a state trooper whose determination and thoroughness is in marked contrast to some of his peers.

There has been no shortage of suspects, including the man who owed Gross money and had gone to great lengths to establish an alibi about where he was the night of the murder. A lie-detector test given this suspect was said to be inconclusive while some other suspects apparently passed.

The trooper subsequently assigned to the case has been unable to find any physical evidence such as traces of Gross's blood at the site of either the burned cottage or the private residence that could lead to an arrest, but believes the murder can be solved.

That will have to wait. The investigator had worked the case for eight years, only to be taken off of it when he was transferred to another barracks. The file was reopened several years later when the investigator was assigned to look into cold cases, but he recently was promoted and under the arcane state police bureaucracy it was more important to his higher ups to transfer him to yet another barracks than keep a fire lit under a homicide investigation that finally seemed to be panning out.

And so Gross's long-suffering parents must endure another indignity at the hands of the state police: An investigation that was half-assed at the start only to be resuscitated by a hands-on trooper who was then reassigned despite the progress he was making only to be put back on the case years later and then be forced to hand it off to an inexperienced young trooper when he was promoted.

Was this done deliberately? Had some unseen hand earmarked the Gross murder to never be solved?

Chapter Thirteen:

ALL HAIL CAESAR!

This story ultimately lacks a hero because the hero died in the first chapter. But it does have plenty of villains, including the most powerful man in the Poconos over a 30-year period during which violent crime spiraled out of control.

That would be James R. Marsh, who was Monroe County district attorney, a county judge and finally county president judge. (A nephew, James F. Marsh, was the prosecutor in the Harry Read murder.)

James R. Marsh wielded power like a cudgel. There was nothing subtle or nuanced about his demeanor and he was extraordinarily vain, so much so that he refused to sit at a lunch counter or bar with mere mortals, always insisting on a chair at a table.

"Do you know what a pyramid is?" he once asked a lawyer who was late for court because he was delayed at a district justice's court. "I am the top and the DJ's are the bottom. Next time you come to the top on time."

As district attorney Marsh had the final say in what criminal cases were pursued, how aggressively they were pursued, or whether they should be pursued at all. That is well within a DA's purview, but Marsh's imperiousness continued unchecked when he became a judge.

A law-enforcement veteran says that Marsh was the de facto commander of the state police barracks at Swiftwater.

"He set the tone for many major investigations," the veteran said. "There would be a high-profile crime and the sergeant at Swiftwater would call him up to see how his men should proceed."

This extraordinary ethical breach helps explain the chronic indifference that the state police showed if a murder victim, like Eddie and the others, was from the wrong side of the tracks.

Marsh was never wrong, and when he erred it was quickly cover up.

As a judge, he president over the trial of a young man who was busted for a small marijuana patch behind his house on federal land in the footprint of the Tocks Island dam project. Marsh demonized the defendant and the proceedings were front page news in the *Pocono Record*. The young man was found guilty, of course. Marsh scheduled the sentencing -- and likely imprisonment -- two weeks hence. The two weeks came and went and then two months. It was not until nearly two years later that the young man learned that someone had whispered to Marsh after the trial that as a county judge he did not have jurisdiction over federal property, but rather than admit to his error and declare a mistrial, Marsh just quietly let the matter drop.

The author of Marsh's 2003 obituary in the *Record* hinted at the aspects of Marsh that people only whispered about in noting that he was "complex," and as DA he was deeply involved in – some would say interfered in – several criminal cases that had a common denominator: They involved gay men either as perpetrators or victims, or men he claimed were gay.

The most pungent example is the Edward Maps murder case.

In January 1962 when Marsh was a young assistant district attorney, he steamrolled the investigation into the deaths of the wife and infant child of Maps, a 39-year-old artist and Korean War veteran, in their Stroudsburg home. Christine Wolbach Maps, 22, had been bludgeoned with some kind of blunt instrument and died later from a skull fracture and cerebral hemorrhage, while four-month-old

Julie Louise Maps died of smoke inhalation after numerous small fires were set in different rooms of the house.

Marsh declared that Maps had killed his wife and set the fires because he was gay, the implication being that homosexuals were so perverted that they would stoop to murdering their loved ones. There was not a shred of evidence for the allegation and it became obvious that Maps had met with foul play and had not, as Marsh claimed, fled and eluded a police dragnet.

Marsh lobbied hard to get Maps on the FBI's Most Wanted List and finally succeeded. Then a year later he asked the bureau to remove Maps from the list.

He never explained why, but it is possible that he became aware that Robert Wolbach, Maps' father-in-law, who had strenuously opposed his daughter's marriage, had arranged for the wife and child of the son-in-law he so loathed to be hurt but not killed by hit men who would kill Maps.

Indeed, crime-scene evidence that Marsh only superficially examined pointed to professionals who intended to kill Maps, whose cars were still in the driveway of the family home, and only injure the wife and child but got carried away. Meanwhile, visitors to Wolbach's farm north of the Stroudsburgs said that among the occasional visitors were ferocious looking men who wore dark suits and sunglasses and drove black Cadillacs with New York state license plates. Not the kind of acquaintances one would expect for a man who by vocation was an art teacher and had became art supervisor for New York City public schools.

Marsh never bothered to pursue other motives, let alone determine whether Wolbach should be a suspect because of his very public hatred of Maps. Maps' body was never found, although there were rumors that weights had been tied to his body and it was disposed of at the bottom of a lake or river.

Meanwhile, Marsh shared a secret with Dr. Nelson: Although also married with children, he too was a closeted homosexual.

While this was an open secret, it was one that Marsh ferociously guarded. His rendezvous with gay men were sometimes arranged at The Back Door, a small private lounge behind Hans Hunsicker's Blue Bugle that was entered from an alley just off Courthouse Square in Stroudsburg where Marsh had offices as DA and judge. The rendezvous often took place in Atlantic City or New York City.

Marsh's sociopathy is reminiscent of J. Edgar Hoover, the legendarily ruthless FBI director who it is claimed also was a closeted homosexual, as well as a cross dresser, and used false allegations of homosexuality against his enemies.

The ability to be generous and fair toward others is not diminished in many people who hide their gayness. Marsh, however, was always conscious of the power he wielded and that he could get away with being malicious and punitive.

It is therefore not surprising that when Eddie's murder investigation foundered and Marsh was petitioned to convene an investigative grand jury and a coroner's inquest in light of the fact that there was an ax murderer on the loose in the Poconos, he rejected both requests.

Chapter Fourteen:

THE HIKER RETURNS

After walking away from The Bottom of the Fox in August 1977, it had taken Owen Owen two months to reach the southern end of the Appalachian Trail. It would be four years before he would try to make good on his pledge to also hike the trail from south to north.

The Irishman was older if not necessarily wiser as he slogged across the crest of the Kittatinny Ridge on the second day of December 1981. He definitely was colder. Setting out from Georgia on his northward trek in October had been foolish. There were few hikers to commiserate with and the nights had grown longer and increasingly bitter.

Three days before Eddie's murder, a driving snowstorm that turned to rain had driven him off the trail and to a motel in a small town in rural Maryland. It was Thanksgiving Day, but everything was closed and his holiday meal consisted of sodden trail food and crackers from a vending machine. He had an inexplicable craving for parkin, a gingerbread made from oatmeal and treacle that he would dunk in tea during late night study sessions at university and hadn't eaten since. For the first time in his life, he fell asleep feeling hunger pangs.

At least it was sunny, if muddy underfoot, as he caught the first glimpse of the Gap.

A day seldom passed when Owen Owen did not look back on his brief interlude at the Fox with deep fondness. Although he could be a shameless embellisher, he had told the story of the bar and its crazy crew without adding any touches during his world travels. Why bother to exaggerate when there were characters like these?

He had corresponded with Glenn Fisher, sending him a stream of letters and postcards from various ports of call in his determined effort to not grow up. Fisher's replies were far less frequent, and his last letter – actually a brief note in the little man's meandering copperplate hand telling him of Eddie's death but not the circumstances -- would lay unopened in a pile of mail addressed to him in the library of his parents' Dublin home for several weeks.

The thought of once again heading down Main Street, grabbing that big antler door handle and walking into the welcoming embrace of the Fox had sustained Owen Owen, as well as made him determined to make his return in backpacker's mufti and not a taxicab, something for which he knew the regulars would unmercifully tease him.

"Didja take that cab all the way from Atlanta, young man?"

And:

"Didja hear the one about the hiker going into the gun store?"

Owen Owen, of course, would play along and said that he hadn't.

"The hiker asks the salesman what kind of handgun he should carry in case he runs into a bear.
"The salesman says, 'Carry any handgun you want. But if you're going to shoot a bear with it, be sure to grind off the front sight.'

On cue, Owen Owen would ask why.

"That way it won't hurt too bad when the bear takes it away and shoves it up the hiker's ass.'"

Yes, they'd have a million of them. And Bob's your uncle.

While Eddie's murder investigation was a sorry affair, his autopsy was first rate.

His corpse had been wheeled into the examination room at the Sacred Heart Hospital morgue in Allentown down in the Lehigh Valley two days after the murder and two days before Owen Owen's arrival. Present were Dr. Isadore Mihalkis, who was the Lehigh County medical examiner, morgue diener Wayne Snyder, Monroe County Coroner Allen, state police detectives Mastruzzo and Mazyurkiewecz, and Gap Police Chief Snow.

Mihalakis was and is one of the best in the business, a much-in-demand forensic pathologist. His post-mortem examination was by the book and not unexpectedly found that Eddie had died from "massive craniocerebral injuries" that included "compound, comminuted, depressed fractures of the skull, dural lacerations and mild bilateral subdural hemorrhage, cerebral lacerations and contusions with intracerebral and traumatic subarachnoid hemorrhage." In other words, he had suffered repeated blows from what in all likelihood was an ax.

As Owen Owen left the ridgeline, followed the trail markers beneath a canopy of hemlocks down to a side street and then Main Street, he suddenly felt the darkness of the mountain.

He broke his trot, slowed to a walk and then stopped as he

replayed in his mind the going-away party in his honor at the Fox, a bittersweet occasion dampened by the news that the body of David Gross had been found that morning at a nearby overlook, as well as Eddie's admonition that Owen Owen's awestruck first impressions of the Poconos to the contrary, all was not sweetness and light. That night had ended on a rowdy note as he and the crew tried to drink away the shock of Gross's murder. Chief Snow had stopped by twice to shush the crowd because of complaints from next door.

Owen Owen shook off the memories and resumed his trot, but the darkness intruded again. Several crows were careering overhead and cawing raucously. The hiker wondered if they were the same posse that Eddie had pointed out in the giant sycamore behind the Fox. They seemed to be alerting him to something that at first he did not understand.

Then he suddenly did. Main Street was not the sleepy scene he had replayed over and over in his mind but was packed with people. He caught a glimpse of Fisher standing at the door of the Presbyterian Church of the Mountain. It stuck him that he and the people pressed around him looked like bees at the mouth of a hive. It was, as he soon learned, a memorial service for Eddie.

"The service was a celebration of Joubert himself," wrote

Joe Middleton, a journalist and jazz lover. "His friends believed this is how Ed would have wanted it -- a joyful event instead of a mournful one."

Owen Owen slipped through the church doors. Conscious of his shabby dress and the fact he hadn't bathed in six days, he stood in the back next to Fisher and together they surveyed a nave so thick with people that they spilled out into the foyer and a room behind the altar.

There were, among many others, Fox family members Robbie Asmus, Kate Holmes, Bill Reinhart, Joanne Jones, Teddy Platt, Linda Fogel, Joe Keiper, Ray Meehan, Darryl Pierson and Bill Giese.

Then there was Rosalie Sorrels, Bill Snow, Dotsie Hauser, Robbie Rosenblum, Anne Davies, Hans Hunsicker, Steve Jackabowitz, Jay Thurman, Ronnie Heller, and of course, Cheryl Joubert and her brothers, sister and mother.

The service opened with the singing of songs and hymns, including "Nature Boy" by Richie Roche. Phil Woods soloed on My Buddy," while Jerry Harris brought the house down with an electrifying "Amazing Grace." There were several numbers by a thrown-together ensemble led by Woods that included Rick Chamberlain, Pat Dorian,

Steve Gilmore, Tony Marino, Michelle Bennett, Bud Nealy, Wolfgang Knittel and Jim Daniels. Reverend Cohea finally climbed the steps to the altar and raised his arms to silence the congregants before beginning to read a moving if meandering tribute to his friend titled "A Man of Many Seasons." (See Appendix One.)

As Cohea closed, Woods led his band in a New Orleans-style funeral march down the aisle, out of the church and down Main Street to the Fox, where a black-trimmed wreath hung near a beer sign in the front window. More than one marcher, exhausted from the long days and longer nights of mourning since Eddie's murder, remarked that they might not have made it if they had to walk uphill.

Eddie was cremated and his ashes placed in a container that sat behind the bar for some time while Cheryl Joubert and her father's friends pondered what should be done with them.

In the end it was decided to scatter the ashes at several of the places around the adopted home that Eddie had loved so deeply, including Sunfish Pond, Smithfield Beach on the Delaware River where he swam, and a slope behind the Minisink Hotel on River Road where he liked to sit atop a huge boulder and ponder the ways of the world.

Mihalakis had found something else of note during the autopsy: Eddie's right kidney was cancerous and there was a large tumor on his liver, something that he would have been unaware of until it was too late since he never went to a doctor. Left undiagnosed, Eddie's odyssey likely would have ended well before his life expectancy had a homicidal maniac not intervened.

AFTERWORD

Back in the day, the astonishing level of violence in the Poconos would not have been particularly noticeable to a day tripper or weekend skier. Nor was it to the people who should have noticed.

That violence was visited upon homeowners and farmers who lived in the Minisink, to sensitive wetlands, cranberry bogs and native fauna as a result of rampant development, and to first-time homeowners who answered the siren call of rapacious developers and mortgage companies and ended up back in the Bronx foreclosed on, broke and broken. Every area has its growing pains, but in the case of the Poconos the very state legislators and county commissioners who swore to represent the best interests of their constituents aided and abetted these serial abuses. None of that can be undone, nor is the "gigantic sewer pipe," as that rueful politician called Interstate 80, going to suddenly dry up.

And while the crime rate in most Pennsylvania counties has remained fairly stable or dropped during the past decade, that rate has soared to epidemic proportions in Monroe County, which experienced a 41 percent leap in adult crimes from 2000 to 2008 compared to a 13 percent increase statewide.

Then there were more personal forms of violence.
In the course of researching *The Bottom of the Fox*, I came across no fewer than 10 individuals in addition to Eddie Joubert who were murdered, died under questionable circumstances, or took their own lives. Extraordinarily, eight of these 10 unexpected passings took place in or within hailing distance of the Gap or involved individuals who were related to Eddie or had lived in the rented rooms at the Fox or Rumours, which is the name that Bobby Stetler gave his discotheque (after a girlfriend's favorite Fleetwood Mac album) when he bought the Fox from Cheryl Joubert in 1984.

Even more extraordinary was the carnage to the families and friends of Eddie and Stetler.

In addition to Eddie's death, there was the suspicious death of one of his sons and the suicide of his brother and one of his brother's sons, as well as the suicides of two of the people to whom he rented rooms, and the murder of David Gross, who was a patron.

Stetler, an All-American soccer player and excellent driver, was killed in a car crash widely believed to not be an accident because the driver's side seat belt of his BMW 325i was cut in an apparent warning to him and then two days later his brake lines were tampered with, which may have caused the fatal crash. Stetler's friend Rory Mahoney was found face down and very dead, his pants around his ankles, in Cherry Creek about a quarter mile upstream from Rumours, while one of Stetler's most trusted employees died in one of his rented rooms.

I do not suggest that there is something inherent in the character of this village of 500 or so people that provoked such carnage, that a mere 75 miles from New York City, a place that many people associate with violence, exists "a killing zone," as one longtime Poconos resident puts it.

It may merely be a statistical anomaly, but if so it is an amazing example of one. By way of comparison, those Gap-related deaths would have translated into a jaw-dropping 6,300 deaths if they took place in the New York City borough of Staten Island, which over the same period had about 700 times the Gap's population.

Very few people are able to look beyond their own relationships with these victims, but many of them speak of an inexplicable "darkness" that seems to descend on the Gap. Some residents joke that the carnage is because of the village's marginally drinkable water. One of Bill Snow's successors as police chief acknowledges that "some pretty messed up things have gone on around here," but like others is unable to put his finger on why. In this context, the contention that the Fox and Rumours were haunted because they were on the site of an Indian burial ground doesn't seem so far fetched. Then there was the business that opened after Stetler's parents sold Rumours. It was gutted by fire.

In addition to the murders and unexplained deaths, there also have been an unusual number of arson fires in the Gap that continue to the present day.

I did the last interview for the first edition of *The Bottom of the Fox* at the Water Gap Diner. Exactly one week later, there was another arson: The longtime owner, who had been sitting near me at the cash register, died of severe burns after fire engulfed his apartment behind the diner. The fire has been declared an arson-homicide, and it is believed that the owner was knocked unconscious and robbed of the large sums of money he was known to keep in the apartment. The fire was set beneath the apartment's steps before the perpetrator fled.

As we have seen, some of this violence resulted from a law enforcement and legal system that was dysfunctional from the highest levels on down.

That too cannot be undone, although a directive from the

governor or state police superintendent to reopen the moribund investigations into the unsolved murders and other questionable deaths would at least be a course correction. The apostates at the Pennsylvania State Police are especially deserving of scorn. While there are doubtless fine officers like the trooper who is so determined to bring Gross's killer to justice, the department has historically been and remains mired in a seemingly irreparable culture of political favoritism, misogyny, cover-ups and scandal.

The investigative work in the four deaths discussed at length in *The Bottom of the Fox* ranged from lackadaisical to unprofessional. The daughter of the state police officer who supervised homicide investigations for Swiftwater and several other northeastern Pennsylvania barracks bitterly complained after reading the first edition of this book that her father was "very concerned" about Eddie's murder, but if that was the case he was at best ineffectual or at worst a liar. One detective is deserving of special scorn because he has tried to wish the truth away by claiming to friends that "some motorcycle guy in California" had confessed to Eddie's murder before he conveniently died.

The same can be said of how the deaths of Stetler and Mahoney were treated. Stetler's car crash was classified as an accident, not a suspicious death as it should have been, while Mahoney's passing was called an apparent suicide when it obviously was not. There is a pattern here: The state police themselves classified and pressed authorities to classify questionable deaths as accidents or suicides, which enabled them to walk away from cases that should have gotten intense scrutiny.

It is difficult to rationalize that how these deaths were handled were aberrations and not more the norm for a law enforcement culture that has seemed more interested in kicking the can down the road than taking killers off the street. The message sent an evildoer in Monroe County during the period that this book covers was emphatic: There was a pretty good chance that you could get away with murder if your victim was someone like Eddie.

Have things changed since then? Hardly.

When I began research for *The Bottom of the Fox* in 2002, the state police were fighting several sexual harassment allegations, one involving a trooper who assaulted a woman in her hospital bed who had attempted suicide. Millions of dollars in settlement money was paid out to the victims. As I finished this book nearly eight years later, the state police were fighting an allegation that a lieutenant was harassed repeatedly after he refused a major's orders to use police computers to snoop on the new beau of the major's estranged wife.

In between, there have been scandals involving inaccurate

state police radar guns that the department hid rather than corrected, shoddy testing at its crime lab, a successful lawsuit after it bungled the investigation of a trooper accused of molesting two girls, the unprecedented demotion of a captain by two ranks because it was falsely believed that he had leaked an internal memo to a newspaper, and the dismissal and subsequent forced rehiring of its highest-ranking woman officer for filing an internal-affairs complaint against a captain.

The *coup de grâce* for me, as it were, came when I was doing fact checking shortly before the first edition of this book went to press, and put in a request with the information office at state police headquarters in Harrisburg to confirm the status of the investigation into Eddie's murder. Which is to say confirm that it was as cold as a midwinter night in the Poconos.

Repeated follow-up calls elicited a range of excuses about why this simple piece of information was not forthcoming, and after five weeks I had to threaten to go higher ups if my request was not answered. It finally was, and the case is indeed as cold as a midwinter night in the Poconos.

How cold is that? A subsequent query revealed that the commander of the Swiftwater barracks asserts that unsolved murder cases such as Eddie's are assigned to troopers who are required to spend some time each year on them. But Eddie, it seems, did not make the cut. This is borne out by family members, Fox employees, friends and law enforcement officials whom I interviewed who stated that they were not aware of any state police activity whatsoever regarding Eddie's case over the past 28 years.

The state police, in fact, treated Eddie's murder as a big joke.

In addition to "the ax fell off the roof" quip that a cab driver conveyed to Kate Holmes, another state police *bon mot* is brought up by Gap old timers when they talk about Eddie's murder. It goes something like this:

"He was chopping down a rubber tree and the ax bounced back and hit him in the head. Oh, and the ax head broke off and rolled down the hill into Cherry Creek where a fish swallowed it and swam out into the ocean."

Ha, ha, ha, ha.

In the end, there were two horrific crimes committed in the Gap in 1981.

There was, of course, Eddie's murder. Although there were people who believed that the best hippie was a dead hippie and said as much, his death was mourned by many Gap residents who had gotten beyond his long hair and the menagerie that bellied up to the bar at the Fox.

He had arrived in a struggling community at precisely the time that there was an emerging confluence of energies that many old timers at first feared and some never were able to accept: The squatters who had come down valley from Tocks, the Vietnam veterans who had come home from a distant war, the arts and crafts people who were attracted to the quaint storefronts on Main Street, and the jazz musicians for whom the area became an adopted home.

Eddie didn't preside over this confluence, but his reach was outsized and then some because of his many projects and causes, from the jazz festival to reaching into his pocket no matter how strapped he might be to find a few bucks for someone who was down on their luck. The Gap owed Eddie a lot, but he never tried to collect.

People in the Poconos may get the politicians they deserve – the officials who have been partners in the destruction of a once special place -- but they don't vote for the state police.

For Eddie's family and close friends, his murder was devastating and senseless in the extreme. Some people live in fear to this day. As if that is not bad enough, this community was victimized a second time by those parties of neglect -- the political and law enforcement establishment, most notably the state police -- who reacted to his death with a practiced yawn.

Eddie and they deserved better.

Appendix One:

'A MAN OF MANY SEASONS'

Following is the text of "A Man For All Seasons," a eulogy written and delivered by the Reverend William Cohea at a memorial service for Eddie Joubert on December 2, 1981, at the Presbyterian Church of the Mountain in Delaware Water Gap, Pennsylvania.

Father, Brother, Friend – Clown of God.

Eddie – Child like Spring. Whimsical, playful.

Sensitive as a queen spout. Caring as a warm summer breeze. Open. A listener. Accepting. But also "one way" like Corrigan. Dedicated to the underdog. Sometimes sounded like dedication to "class war" with an Alinski Style all his own.

A Dreamer. Schemer. A worker. What a worker. Believed in change. Had visions of a new society. Childlike. What a worker. Man-like in scheme. If he could not change the Water Gap he turned his energies on the Fox. Move the bar. Turn it around. Cut it in half. No wall was safe! Loud musicians. "His kind of people." And music he had!

A People Man. Giving others the benefit of doubt. Took them in. Gave money to all. Was used. Gave people a second, third and fourth chance. Loved. Cared. He also knew how to kick ass.

Many a time in consultation, conference. Rap with Eddie. Or

whatever one calls a session with Eddie. He'd say "Cohea, I'm going to send them up the hill to you." My response would be: "Eddie, you're soft like a mother. And you ask me to be father. Other times I'd say come up with them ... or why give me the over the hill ones?

He dreamed that this would be an open community. Believed if people worked together it could happen, ie., the Gazebo, The Wiz were collaborations. Even the Chamber of Commerce when elected Treasurer. It was an ironic day for Eddie. High Value on everyone doing "their thing." He became a hippie after it went out of style. That's courage!

A Yankee Trader from fine wood to clams. Soft as a summer breeze and hard as winter freeze.

Up, up and away, Ed. Not ready? But who is?

Some December Reflections on clowning, The Gap and those who come here to be or do their thing: This gathered group today has enough theological independence to cause God to resign. Let alone the clergy, priest and rabbi.

What is it with The Gap? A clowning ground for being like a Giant Magnet, it calls the creative, the sensitivities, the spiritually inclined. There is an Energy in the mountain range. Ancient, powerful, releasing. But also a "no-nonsense" energy. So we come here. Touched, called, prompted. Here there is a "release of energy" which flows forth in creativity, effervescence, dreams, hopes, visions. Music! But energy that is not focused and grounded gets wasted. Burns people out.

It's like the man who had a house wired for 110 and heard of 220 and wanted it.

Called Met Ed. Refused. Fought with Met Ed. Normal. Finally out of exasperation 220 brought to the house. He, of course, said he had rewired. He sneaks out at night. Connects. Goes in and turns on the lights. Burns out. Too many times in The Gap with all its energy and power is tapped, but we have not prepared our own selves to carry the current of energy and there is Burnout. Because we fail to take the time or pay the cost to rewire. To ground ourselves. Our lives. After Burnout we get our spiritual highs in other ways and the energies of The Gap are once more used. And confused. Become Gap Clones. Looks, no Spirit. When I walk up the trail I feel the energies reflected in the stones. Hurt, withdrawn, downcast, waiting for the children of The Gap to grow up. To take on responsibility and accountability of being Co-Creators of the New Creation with Full Energy and Flow. That's what clowning is about.

But a clown has fallen. Call it Karma, Reincarnation, Spirit. Call life a Divine obstacle course. All these calls make God a scapegoat. When we affirm we are of the Divine image, each one called to be clowns of God, we are to unfold to the fullness of the flower we are in His endless energies. We are sons and daughters in and of the Divine Image. Clown of God. When released from this body we are off for more schooling or retooling so that the new creation which Christ is about. Christ the verb of God. The active Energy of God. Can be completed in us and in all of Creation.

We are not to be Clones of Religion or of Culture of The Gap. Called to be Clowns of God. Heirs of life. Dedicated Clowns. Focused, grounded, playful. To Eddie: A Clown of God. Winter, spring, summer or fall. We wish you a good show, you Reluctant Saint.

Appendix Two:

MURDER THEORIES

I put forward the theory that Eddie Joubert was murdered because he had learned of the existence of a sado-masochistic sex ring, its possible link to several murders and that ring members knew that he was onto them. Pennsylvania State Police investigators believed that his death was drug-related, while family, friends and Bottom of the Fox patrons had a number of other theories. They included:

ANACONDA LINK: A man calling himself "The Anaconda" had made threatening phone calls to the Fox, a Joubert family member and a Fox employee.

DEBT LINK: It was suggested that Eddie may have own someone or some organization money and had not paid it back.

INDIAN LINK I: Two Passamaquoddy Indians from Maine who had stayed at the Fox were said to have stolen cash and guns from Eddie and may have returned.

INDIAN LINK II: Eddie would sometimes talk about apparently secret Indian rituals that he claimed to be privy to. Might these Indians have wanted to silence him?

JEALOUS SPOUSE LINK: Eddie was romantically involved with several married women. Might a jealous spouse have come after him?

ORGANIZED CRIME LINK: Eddie had quit his job as a Teamsters Union organizer in disgust because the Russell Bufalino crime family had infiltrated the union's North Jersey locals. Might a mafiosi have come after him?

PINBALL LINK: Eddie was said to have beaten a hustler in a high-stakes pinball game at the Fox. Did the hustler seek revenge?

MUSIC ROYALTIES LINK: Eddie refused to pay royalties to ASCAP for the songs by copyrighted artists that bands performing at the Fox played. An employee says she once received a call from a man who threatened to kill Eddie if he didn't start playing royalties.

Appendix Three:

'DEATH DON'T HAVE NO MERCY'

The deaths of these individuals are discussed in The Bottom of the Fox or are related to individuals and places discussed in the book:

BRUCE MANN (Died April 18, 1974) -- This gay man was found dead of a gunshot wound behind his Pocono Summit apartment after alerting friends that if anything happened to him a prominent community leader and member of a gay sex ring would know who killed him. His death was ruled a suicide despite substantial evidence to the contrary.

DAVID ALLEN GROSS (Died August 10, 1977) -- The young marijuana dealer was found dead in the back of his car at a scenic overlook near the village of Delaware Water Gap after cashing a check made out to him by the prominent community leader and member of the gay sex ring and then being ambushed in the course of making a large marijuana deal. His murder remains unsolved.

EDDIE JOUBERT (Died November 28, 1981) -- The owner of the Bottom of the Fox in the Gap was found dead of multiple ax wounds on a cellar ramp behind his bar. He may have learned of the existence of the gay sex ring as well as the perpetrators in one or more of the murders linked to members of the ring. His murder remains unsolved.

RORY MAHONEY (Died 1984) -- The best friend of Bobby Stetler, who bought The Bottom of the Fox in 1983 and renamed it Rumours, was found dead face down in Cherry Creek in the Gap. His pants were pulled down around is ankles. His death was ruled a suicide despite substantial evidence to the contrary.

HARRY REED (Died March 31, 1985) -- This owner of two gay bars was found dead of multiple stab wounds on Pensyl Creek Road in Hamilton Township the morning after he sold one of his businesses to another prominent member of the gay sex ring but before he had been paid. A young man was arrested and convicted of the murder but police never pursued the motive.

BILL GIESE (Died April 9, 1987) -- This troubled Vietnam veteran and former resident of a second-floor room at the Bottom of the Fox killed himself with a handgun in a bedroom of his mother's Stroudsburg home.

PHILIP JOUBERT (Died February 15, 1990) -- The brother of Eddie Joubert and part owner of the Bottom of the Fox was despondent about his failed marriage and hung himself at his Middle Smithfield Township home. His body was found by his son, Shawn Joubert.

BOBBY STETLER (Died July 29, 1990) -- The owner of Rumours, formerly the Bottom of the Fox, was found dead after being thrown from his BMW coupe at a railroad crossing on River Road near the Gap. Investigators ruled that the crash was an accident, but friends state that his driver's side seat belt had been cut two days before the crash, which may have been caused by the car's brake lines being intentionally cut.

JAMES JOUBERT (Died early 1990s) -- The older of Eddie Joubert's two sons was living in a halfway house in Williamport, Pennsylvania when a fight broke out at a party he was attending. Family members say that a partygoer jumped him and choked him to death, then tried to cover up the crime as a drug overdose.

DAN SNYDER (Died October 10, 1994) -- This former resident of a second-floor room at the Bottom of the Fox allegedly had been caught embezzling money from the bingo fund of the Delaware Water Gap Volunteer Fire Company. He was found dead next to his car off of River Road near the Gap after he apparently put a quarter stick of dynamite in his mouth and lit the fuse.

KEITH JOUBERT (Died August 19, 1998) -- The younger son of Phil Joubert, Eddie Joubert's brother and a 1990 suicide victim, hung himself from a rafter in a garage behind the Nanticoke, Pennsylvania home of older son Shawn Joubert, who had found his father's body.

ABOUT THE AUTHOR

Shaun D. Mullen is an award-winning journalist and blogger.

Among the stories Mullen covered over a 35-year newspaper career were the Vietnam War, O.J. Simpson murders and trials, Clinton impeachment circus and coming of Osama bin Laden and Al Qaeda. He also mentored young reporters who have gone on to be among the best in the newspaper and television news businesses, including two who were awarded Pulitzer Prizes in 2010.

Five of the stories and investigative series that he supervised were nominated for Pulitzer Prizes, including exposes on the infiltration of organized crime into Atlantic City building trades and casino unions, the malfeasance of the Pennsylvania State Medical Board, and The Six Hundred Thirty: The Stories of Philadelphia's Vietnam War Dead, biographies of all of the men from Philadelphia who died or went missing in Vietnam.

Mullen currently blogs at *Kiko's House* and is a guest contributor at *OpinionEditorial*, among other blogs.

ON THE WEB

For further information, updates or to leave a comment about *The Bottom of the Fox*, go to www.bottomofthefox.com

One dollar from the sale of each copy of *The Bottom of the Fox* will be donated to the Delaware Water Gap Celebration of the Arts. To make a direct donation, go to www.cotajazz.org

Made in the USA
Charleston, SC
03 September 2010